HERE'S
a proved  publicity feature!
—THE TIE-UP BETWEEN YOUR STORE, THE THEATRE AND JANTZEN

THE HIT OF THE SEASON
☆
NAME OF PICTURE
FEATURING
LORETTA YOUNG
WARNER BROS.-FIRST NATIONAL STAR

A great show! Packed with the finest entertainment of the year —starring delightful Loretta Young. You'll like her. You'll like the Jantzen Shouldaire she always wears too. You will find its mate and all the new Jantzens at (NAME OF STORE)

NAME OF THEATRE

Many merchants have used the theatre-store publicity tie-up during the past two years with marked success. We have broadened its scope for 1932 and recommend its use as an excellent means of securing widespread publicity. Through an exclusive arrangement which we have made with Warner Bros.-First National Pictures, several of their featured artists are available for tie-up publicity. Your local theatre manager will call on you when films featuring these artists are scheduled for his theatre. He will be ready to cooperate with you in every possible way for your mutual advantage. His displays and his advertising will work for you. Yours will help him.

We will furnish you and the theatre manager with newspaper mats for a tie-up advertising campaign. Your advertisements, appearing on the regular pages, will feature Jantzen suits being worn by Warner Bros.-First National star, your store as headquarters and will mention the picture and theatre in the copy. (See specimen store ads on the right.) The theatre advertisements on the theatrical page will feature the artists and picture and mention your store name in the copy. (See specimen theatre ads on the left.) Lobby and billboard displays will be used by the theatre in their cooperative work with you.

"WHO WOULDN'T CHOOSE THE Jantzen
SHOULDAIRE"
SAYS LORETTA YOUNG

If you want a smart sun-suit—and an ideal swimming suit—all in one—ask for the Shouldaire. Loretta Young, the sensational Warner Bros.-First National star of (name of picture) now playing at (name of theatre) is an ardent Jantzen devotee. She has found, as you will find, that a Jantzen is always correct—always fits perfectly and permanently.

NAME OF STORE

BE SURE TO SEE
JOAN BLONDELL
IN THE WARNER BROS.-FIRST NATIONAL
NAME OF PICTURE

A sensation! One of the greatest pictures of the year, featuring that sparkling star— Joan Blondell. How she wears her clothes —as smartly as she wears this Jantzen Formal. ● You'll find this suit, by the way, at (NAME OF STORE)

NAME OF THEATRE

LORETTA YOUNG STATUETTE

A striking piece of display material for interior or window trim. Lithographed in nine colors — 37 inches high. Theatres will have these statuettes for lobby display. They will be furnished to you without cost. Use order blank enclosed.

"I PREFER THE NEW Jantzen FORMAL"
SAYS JOAN BLONDELL

As smartly styled as a Paris gown; the new Jantzen Formal! An invisible tie assures a perfect-fitting back. No wonder Joan Blondell— featured star in Warner Bros.-First National picture, (name of picture), now playing at (name of theatre) prefers it. We're showing all the new Jantzens now —they're worth seeing.

NAME OF STORE

Let's Go to the Beach

A History of Sun and Fun by the Sea

ELIZABETH VAN STEENWYK

Henry Holt and Company
New York

"Everything told of the sea . . ."

—from *Cape Cod*
by Henry David Thoreau

Henry Holt and Company, LLC
Publishers since 1866
115 West 18th Street
New York, New York 10011

Henry Holt is a registered trademark
of Henry Holt and Company, LLC

Library of Congress Cataloging-in-Publication Data
Van Steenwyk, Elizabeth.
Let's go to the beach: a history of sun and fun by the sea /
by Elizabeth Van Steenwyk.
p.   cm
Includes bibliographical references (p.).
1. Beaches—United States—Recreational use—History—
Juvenile literature.   2. Outdoor recreation—United
States—Juvenile literature.   3. Beaches—United States—
Miscellanea—Juvenile literature.   [1. Beaches.
2. Outdoor recreation.]   I. Title.
GV191.62 .V25 2001   797—dc21   00-59664

ISBN 0-8050-6235-1
First Edition—2001 / Book design by David Caplan
Printed in the United States of America on acid-free paper. ∞

1 3 5 7 9 10 8 6 4 2

*To the
Stars of my Sand and Sea—*

*Elizabeth, Todd,
Daniel, Gretchen, Michael,
Andrew, Donnie, Aaron, Charlie,
Don Kerry, Emma Kate,
and Andy Maxy*

In Appreciation

I would like to thank the following good people for their stories, insight, and lively interest and support in this project. Each word, each photograph, and all professional assistance is gratefully acknowledged.

Martha Tolles

Nancy Smiler Levinson

Tony Johnston

John Clark

Rex R. Elliott, sand collector and photographer

Lael Littke

Leonard Arrington, Ph.D.

Arthur MacArthur, Jantzen, Inc., Portland, Oregon

Joan T. Morris, Florida State Archives, Tallahassee, Florida

Les and Libby Stockton

Candice Collins-Boden, Chamber of Commerce, Provincetown, Massachusetts

Lillian Tucker

Nancy E. Haggquist

Nicholas D'Errico, Director, International Sand Collectors' Society, North Haven, Connecticut

Elizabeth Gushee, Library of Virginia, Richmond, Virginia

Sarah Ruszcyk, Coney Island, USA

Joe Pecoraro, Manager of Beaches and Pools, Chicago Park District

Barbara Schwarz, Cannon Beach Historical Society, Cannon Beach, Oregon

Anita Duquette, Whitney Museum of American Art, New York City

Katherine Hamilton-Smith, Lake County Museum, Wauconda, Illinois

Anne Easterling, The Museum of the City of New York

Brian Feeny, National Park Service, New York City

Mark Silver

Stuart Silver

Laurie and Bruce Maclin

Stephen Leatherman, Ph.D. (aka Dr. Beach)

Patricia Wuest

Vicki Gold Levi

Sherry Shahan

Carl Price, Atlantic City Public Relations Service

John Kessel, USA Volleyball Association, Denver, Colorado

Claire Lyons, Collections Curator, Research Library, Getty Research
    Institute, Malibu, California

Tracey Schuster, Getty Research Institute

Dennis Harmuth

Glenn Bunting

Mindy Pellissier, Dog Beach Dog Wash

My editor, Christy Ottaviano, deserves a special note of
appreciation. Her advice, enthusiasm, and patience have been
indispensable to this project, and completing it would not have
been possible without her unfailing good cheer at the other
end of the telephone line. Thank you, Christy.

Contents

Introduction

During my teenage years, a time when most young people dream of spending their summers at the beach, I lived in land-locked Illinois. My total seashore experience consisted of pedaling seven miles out to Lake Bracken on my bicycle, where a beach about the size of a soda cracker hugged an old brown-shingled bathing pavilion. Swimmers stepped onto this strip of sand just before they waded into the lake.

Anyone wanting to soak up a few rays after a swim found it easier and safer to relax on one of the two rafts marking the boundaries of the swimming area rather than trying to sun on that minuscule bit of sandy surface. Little kids, swinging pails and shovels, waddled around like dangerous sea urchins, taking more than their share of space. They didn't give anyone a moment's relaxation.

When I discovered there was a real (translate that: large) beach in Chicago at Lake Michigan, my friends and I tried it out. However, I never expected it to be carpeted with so many people! There weren't *that* many people in my hometown.

Thousands of bathers gather at Oak Street Beach against a high-rise background in Chicago; mid-1940s.

From the beginning Chicago has kept its lakefronts available to its citizens for the purpose of enjoying the beach. A plan was initiated so that big buildings could not be built on the lake side of the outer drive, even though they soon crowded the inner side of the drive. It was always amazing to me to turn and see the skyscrapers engulfing the beaches of the city when I had been so used to a skyline of pine trees surrounding my hometown beach.

If my beach experiences were limited as a midwesterner, a friend who grew up in Minneapolis had a more typical beach life in the summertime. Minnesota is known for its ten thousand lakes, and Nancy grew up three blocks from one of them, Lake Harriet. There were four wide and gravelly beaches surrounding this lake. As a young girl she walked to the lake carrying faded old towels and wearing a one-piece suit. She was allowed to swim to the raft, but only one hour after eating, not a moment before. That was the rule then.

As a teenager she swam at Lake Calhoun. This beach in particular was set aside for teenagers who were looking for a date. Few girls swam, because they didn't want to ruin their hairdos. Boys spent their time showing off, revving the motors of their cars or making pyramids by standing on one another's shoulders to display their muscles. Toward the end of August, a lot of pollution had accumulated in the lakes, making them less than attractive to swimmers.

The Taylor sisters enjoy Carpinteria Beach, California; 1949.

With my limited access to oceans, my beach life was short and shallow until I moved to California and discovered the true meaning of those magic words, "Let's go to the beach."

Now I know the attraction, however, and it differs for each person who packs up and heads for a day of sun and fun on the shore. "Let's go to the beach" means just plain sunning to some, surfing to others, searching for bits of flora and fauna, or showing off muscles to gaping admirers. It can also mean a day of serious sports exercise, an eating marathon, or sitting on a beach towel and counting the waves.

Beaches on rivers, lakes, and oceans are now accessible to nearly everyone throughout the world. There are 650 public recreational beaches in the United States alone, and the number is growing all the time.

Many changes have taken place since I was a teenager and

enjoyed summers at my beach. One thing remains the same, and that is the awareness everyone must maintain while spending a day in or near the water. Swimmers have to be alert for the unexpected and know what to do when the unexpected occurs.

Writing this book has been an exciting, exhilarating, and challenging experience. Throughout the process I met many new and interesting people across the United States. One problem began to emerge, however. As I collected material and listened to stories, then followed leads to other experts in their fields, I became aware of how much material there was on the subject. Soon I realized there were too many beaches! How would I ever choose which ones to talk about?

I decided to include a little bit of everything—an overview, a cornucopia of information for my readers. So how to do this? Slowly, my plans took shape. I researched those beaches that were historically important, wrote about others that were world famous, and looked into the social and cultural aspects that beach life offers. I pursued geographical diversity as well.

But there were still lesser known beaches that offered the best surfing, shell collecting, fishing, or simply the sweetest memories for people I'd met. I just had to write about those. In addition, I felt it appropriate and necessary to include safety and environmental information that would be useful to the readers of this book.

Which beaches have been selected? You'll find my choices on the following pages, and I hope your favorite is among them. If not, you may find another one you like equally well. Now—let's go to the beach!

Holly and Lynn Tucker exchange girl talk on Lake Michigan beach at Frankfort, Michigan; 1981.

Let's Go to the Beach

CHAPTER ONE

In the Beginning at the Beach: The Way It Was

"Last one in is a rotten egg!" That challenge is heard at beaches, pools, lakes, and rivers during American summers, and similar versions echo all over the world in other languages. Although it's been said for centuries, no one really knows who coined the term before leaping into the water.

Do we really know what the early inhabitants of Earth thought as they stood on the border between land and water that we now call the beach? Did they wonder about the ocean or river and what was in it or where it led? Did they worry that the land would be swept away with the rise and fall of tides? And more to the subject of this book, when did it occur to early residents that it might be fun to get wet?

Our ancient ancestors used the beach from which to launch boats and search the waters for food vital to survival. Because their crudely made vessels offered little protection, they were soaked

A windy day is a beautiful day on Virginia Beach, Virginia; late 1980s.

by frigid waters and often remained in sodden clothes for long hours, risking the danger of illness. Sometimes they fell overboard and even drowned in pursuit of the food that would feed their families, provide light and fuel and, in some instances, clothe them as well.

The Egyptians were among the first to show the way. The book of Exodus in the Bible tells us that the ancient priests purified themselves by bathing in the sacred waters of the Nile River. The Egyptians also used their waterways as an escape from the enemy.

The Greeks found their surrounding waters beneficial for fishing and as paths to commerce with other countries. When they saw Egyptians relaxing in the Nile, it occurred to them to do likewise at home. Considering it important to cleanse their bodies as well as show them off, Greek men and children soon were bathing regularly in rivers and streams. (No women could be seen in public dressed in clothing that revealed their bodies.) And there's the rubadubdub. The Greeks didn't have any soap as we know it today. So what did they do? They rubbed themselves first with oil and then sand before rinsing the mixture off.

When public baths were built in Greek cities and grew increasingly popular during the fourth century B.C., bathing became strictly a social experience as men flocked to the bathhouses to meet their friends and exchange gossip.

It was a man's world at first. They wore togas to and from the water, be it in bathhouses or in natural bodies of water. Older citizens, especially those with money, wore long linen robes in order to show off their social and financial standing before they immersed themselves.

Herodotus, a Greek historian who wrote a series of nine books called Histories, talked about "bearing our newborn infants to the flood." This idea most likely meant that Greeks began swimming lessons early. The daring of Greek swimmers was not to be denied when they finally tired of their version of hot tubs and began to use their muscles. Swimming against the tides became part of their military training, and it must have worked, too, because soon their armies were the best in the ancient world.

ALONG CAME THE ROMANS

Then it was the Romans' turn to discover the wonders of water. As their own armies strengthened, they conquered Europe, western Asia, and northern Africa. When the Romans eventually overpowered the Greeks, great funds of knowledge were placed in Roman hands. They borrowed many ideas from the Greeks, particularly training their young men to swim. (Swimming was considered strictly a male sport by the Romans as well.) Beginners were placed on floats made of rushes or corks, because it was believed they could use their arms more easily on this kind of support. The sport received high status as a healthy, manly, and useful activity. As the standard of living rose in the Roman Empire, recreational swimming developed in popularity. Elegant swimming pools lined with marble were built adjacent to magnificent homes.

Bathing soon became a daily duty of Roman men and

Italian archaeologist Gino V. Gentili discovered this mosaic—depicting female gymnasts wearing an early version of the bikini—while excavating the fourth-century Roman Villa del Casale, Piazza Amerina, in Sicily.

women, and before long, there were 850 public baths in the city. Some of them were so large that it was said a thousand people could relax in one bath at the same time. Floors were made of mosaic or marble, and walls were often covered with paintings. Men and women lounged in the pool as they read, listened to poets and philosophers orate, and even exercised.

When bathing with the multitudes turned into a standing-room-only event, people quickly found other, less crowded locations to get wet. They moved to rivers, lakes, and the ocean, too.

Romans were passionate about water sports. Young Roman military cadets swam in the Tiber River, which flowed past the Campus Martius, and the sport quickly became part of their training. If anyone can be considered a good example of a military man who knew how to stay afloat, it was Julius Caesar. When Caesar attempted to conquer Egypt, Ptolemy XIII counterattacked at Alexandria. Forced to withdraw from his position on a bridge, Caesar leaped into the sea and swam to his fleet anchored in the harbor.

The story gets better as told by Plutarch, a Greek writer known for his biographies of famous men. (His book *Parallel*

Lives described many important historical events with great dramatic skill, although his accuracy was sometimes doubtful.) In describing Caesar's leap into the sea, Plutarch said, "He was holding many papers in his hand and would not let them go, though missiles were flying at him . . . but he held them with one hand and swam with the other." Another account said that Caesar not only swam with one arm but also dragged his coat through the water by his teeth, so the coat wouldn't fall into enemy hands.

Julius Caesar (100–44 B.C.) enjoyed a brilliant career as a Roman general and statesman, often using his athletic abilities during military campaigns to conquer nearby nations.

As the Romans continued to conquer other countries, they came to an island north of them that looked inviting. The residents of that tiny isle were not hospitable to a takeover, however. When the Romans landed at Kent, England, in A.D. 43 to begin colonization, the British fought back. During the Roman conquest of Great Britain, especially early on when Julius Caesar was involved, swimming was featured in most military campaigns. Soldiers swam, their horses swam, the local citizens swam, and mayors, generals, and emperors swam, especially Caesar. It was said that he "crossed rivers which barred his path by swimming or floating on inflated skins," which must have been forerunners of our floats. Later, William Shakespeare wrote the following lines for Caesar to ask in *Caesar and Cleopatra*:

> Dar'st thus, Cassius now,
> Leap in with me into this angry flood
> And swim to yonder point?

Once the peaceful occupation by Roman soldiers began, public and private baths were established. The village of Bath was already in existence before the Romans arrived, but the conquerors built a reservoir that still stands today. The mineral water that poured from the reservoir was believed to have healing properties. Later, the Romans created artificial swimming pools, although they were not common. But the swimming craze had begun in Great Britain and soon became popular with rich and poor, young and old.

As their empire fell apart in A.D. 476, the Romans lost control of Great Britain and other nearby countries. Coincidence or not, interest in water sports dried up everywhere in Europe, except in Britain. Their next conquerors, the Anglo-Saxons, were swimmers, too, so the tradition continued in Great Britain even into the Norman and Elizabethan periods.

In other parts of Europe, however, as the influence of the Greeks' quest for knowledge and the Romans' search for pleasure ended, the Anglo-Saxons from the north brought reality. Plague, starvation, isolation, fires, and floods got the immediate attention of all the citizens. Swimming and frolicking in the surf suddenly lacked in importance. Even bathing for hygiene and health took a backseat to survival. Intellectual inquiry gave in to the primary needs of the populace, and cleanliness gave way to strange notions about the effects of water on the body. Slowly, a pall settled over what was known as the civilized world. Although that period of time from 450 to 750 is most often called the Dark Ages in history books, it could also be thought of as the Dirty Ages. Getting wet was no longer fun; it was considered downright dangerous to one's well-being. The Greeks were right in the first place. Who needs soap anyway?

THE WORLD WISES UP . . . AND CLEANS UP

Gradually, people of western Europe began to wake up from the economic and intellectual inactivity of the Dark Ages. They looked around, wondered what had happened to the rest of the world. Although most of the Europeans believed the world was flat, a few adventurous folks sailed away to unexplored territory and voila! they didn't fall off. Christopher Columbus, Vasco da Gama, and Ferdinand Magellan were but a few of the explorers who saw life in the New World and rushed home with reports of emerald waters and pristine beaches where native men and women lived seemingly perfect lives.

About this time it must have occurred to the Europeans that they had beaches, too, and perhaps their health could be improved by going there. It wasn't easy to change their way of thinking, however. For hundreds of years both health and hygiene had been ignored by the multitudes. Plagues had devastated Europe in the 1400s and 1500s, and those who survived insisted it was for one reason: they had kept their bodies so well covered that unhealthful vapors couldn't touch their skin, allowing disease to enter their pores. Now they began going to the beach that way—bundled up until it was nearly impossible to identify any one individual.

City dwellers in particular tried everything now to become healthy. They drank foul-tasting waters emitting from springs, they chewed seaweed, and they stuck their toes in the sea. When the English first tried swimming on their seacoasts, they found the waters frigid but invigorating. The water was cleaner, the air smelled better than that in urban areas, and people generally began to feel healthier. They threw off a few layers of clothing, walked and exercised, ate more nutritious foods, and gave full credit to the beach for their improved lives.

The first paper written about swimming came in 1538 from the pen of a Dutchman, Nicolas Wynman. He advised, "Don't bathe at night when toads, snakes and other hurtful things are abroad, . . . and refrain from swimming during the changes of the moon."

Later, in 1759, a British doctor, Richard Russell, published an essay on the uses of seawater for internal and external purposes. Four years later he built a house by the sea at Brighton, England, and originated a strange new practice called strip and plunge. He would hire a strong person, man or woman, to plunge a semiclothed bather into the sea and hold him down until he swallowed a lot of water. Semidrowning was thought to be good for one's health. After all, the patient felt so good when the treatment stopped, he must be healthier. Strangely, people allowed themselves to be treated this way at seaside resorts for days at a time, and even paid for the dubious privilege.

Then along came Vincent Priessnitz with a good story to tell. Traveling around Europe during the early 1800s, he told anyone who'd listen that a wagon accident had left him with broken bones and bruises everywhere. He claimed to have made himself well by dunking himself in ice water. Perhaps he could be seen as the first member of the Polar Bear Club! After he convinced his listeners that he'd found a miracle cure for all his aches and pains, he went home to Grafensberg, in what is now Poland, and opened Water University. Soon, thousands of people arrived to take the cure, make Priessnitz a wealthy man, and refocus attention to an underrated commodity—water.

In England and France, bathing in natural springs for health quickly grew in popularity. It was a public affair; men and women bathed separately. Men wore the same kind of togas the Greeks and Romans had used centuries before. Women wore long gowns with disks of lead sewn into the hems, to prevent their clothing from floating upward and baring their legs. Collections of huts in which to change clothes were put up around natural springs and pools, and the times set for men's use and women's use were announced by a blast on a horn.

The ocean was a natural attraction, and going to the beach quickly became the rage in Great Britain. Apparently its citizens were so invigorated after a plunge in the sea that British armies and navies began to flex their collective muscles and act aggressively on the high seas. Soon, the British found themselves with thirteen colonies in the New World who knew how to act aggressively, too, and wanted their freedom from British rule. But it wasn't going to be easy for the colonists to have their way. The thirteen colonies had beaches up and down their eastern coastlines. Just what King George III and his minions wanted!

CHAPTER TWO

Trails and Rails: Getting There Is Half the Fun

A little more than a hundred fifty years before the thirteen colonies in the New World rebelled, some disgruntled British subjects left home to start lives free of religious persecution. In 1620, this not-so-merry band of English men and women, later called Pilgrims by historians, came ashore in the New World on a wide beach at what is now Provincetown, Massachusetts. The Pilgrims spent five weeks exploring Cape Cod, looking for a good place to settle and put down roots to begin a new government.

Citizens of Provincetown, Massachusetts, re-enact Pilgrims coming ashore during celebrations; October 1997.

Myles Standish wandered farther down the beach to a location that would become Eastham. There he encountered a band of Nauset Indians. Arrows were flung as a warning to the trespassers, and Mr. Standish took the hint. The Pilgrims left and didn't come back to Cape Cod for twenty-four years. By this time they'd met a few friendly faces among the Native Americans at Plymouth on the mainland and established themselves there. When George III began his reign in Great Britain some time later, thirteen colonies in the New World teemed with ideas of self-determination and religious freedom like those of the first Pilgrims.

The thirteen colonies knew there was no question about who owned the beaches on their East Coast as well as everything else in the colonies. *They* did. They were about to settle things once and for all time. In 1776, the political leaders of the colonies came together; Thomas Jefferson wrote the Declaration of Independence, and everyone thought freedom was assured. Not so the British. They summoned their red-coated soldiers, who soon arrived on the colonies' eastern shores to put down the rebellion.

The colonists fought for the beaches and everything else they considered theirs. The fight was no small thing, not ending until 1781, when the redcoats went home. Later, the thirteen colonies elected George Washington their first president and forged a nation. Not long

Martha Dandridge Custis was an attractive twenty-six-year-old widow in 1758 when British artist John Wollaston painted her portrait. In January 1759, she married George Washington, who became the first president of the United States.

afterward, George's wife, Martha, took up the habit of bathing in natural springs, a practice that had come over to the colonies with the redcoats. Naturally, Martha wore the costumes adorned with lead disks. It wouldn't do to have the first First Lady displaying her "limbs."

Soon the new nation needed more room and more roads on which to expand. Before long, the government authorized and encouraged citizens to build them, using waterways when possible. In 1803, Thomas Jefferson, the third president, closed a real estate deal with France called the Louisiana Purchase. He promptly sent Meriwether Lewis and William Clark to lead the Corps of Discovery through this new territory to locate a waterway to the Pacific Ocean. Lewis and Clark explored a network of rivers including the Missouri, Snake, and Columbia that led them, finally, to the beaches of the Pacific. On November 7, 1805, William Clark wrote the immortal words in his field notes, "Ocian [sic] in view! Oh, the joy."

Oh, the mistake! The corps were looking at the Columbian estuary where the river joins the ocean, and they didn't find the ocean itself for several more days. Then Lewis and Clark located a site near the beach and built a fort for shelter. Calling it Fort Clatsop, the party of explorers stayed there through the winter of 1805–1806. On the beach they built a salt-making camp and produced salt by boiling seawater in large kettles. They wanted enough to use during the rest of the winter as well as to carry eastward when they left the following March. Today, visitors can experience this part of the voyage through the reconstruction of both Fort Clatsop and the salt-making camp, the second most important beach in our nation's history.

ON THE MOVE

It was apparent that Lewis and Clark had discovered a major waterway of transportation across the nation, eventually discovering a beach, too. Traveling by land, however, required the knowledge of citizens who were experts and entreprencurs in other forms of locomotion. The first roads linking the small communities of the new nation together were old Indian and animal trails that followed the eastern seashore. As they moved inland, colonists began to hack through thick forests and underground brush to create crude passageways for their wagons.

By the mid-1800s, toll roads came into existence. Travelers paid a toll, or fee, to cover costs to build additional roads that bigger wagons, serving the country's expanding economy, required. As an example, a 297-mile trip between Philadelphia and Pittsburgh lasted for seven rough days and cost seven dollars for food and lodging on the way. Despite the time and expense, the nation and its citizens were on the move.

Railroads began to take off in the United States a little while later. By the 1830s, engines and railroad cars chugged up and down the eastern seaboard, linking one city to another. Passenger service revolutionized travel. People who had never before traveled more than twenty miles from home were seized with a curious yearning to take a trip. The toots of the train whistles beckoned them. All they needed was a destination.

COMES ANOTHER REVOLUTION

The Industrial Revolution began in the United States in the early 1800s as men, women, and children found jobs in factories that were located in developing urban areas. Before, when farmers and laborers worked for themselves, the sun regulated their lives. Now clocks assumed that role. Clocks made new allocations in their days, including time to play as well as work. Over the years more changes occurred. Soon everyone had a block of time called the weekend (although it might be only Sunday), plus occasional vacations if workers could afford them. Reformers even provided playgrounds on factory sites for children who worked twelve-to-fourteen-hour days, so that they could be given short periods of playtime.

The wealthy class already had time for leisure activities. While the British indulged themselves at seaside resorts, the American elite relaxed at promenades and fancy dress balls, and visited one another on weekends. The poorer class amused themselves with outdoor activities such as hunting and fishing, which also produced additional food for their tables.

The World's Columbian Exposition in Chicago in 1893 (also known as the World's Fair) brought about dynamic changes in the public's demand for leisure-time activities. Most of the twenty-one million visitors preferred the section called the Midway to the educational, foreign, and business displays. The Midway featured colorful and exotic attractions, especially dancers doing the hootchy-kootchy, a dance that was considered daring, because the performers wore skimpy clothes and moved in ways that were thought to be suggestive. The Mid-

CONEY ISLAND

The Pennsylvania Steel Company copied the Ferris wheel seen on the Chicago Midway and built this one at Steeplechase Park, Coney Island, in the late 1890s. It was said that its lights could be seen thirty-eight miles at sea.

way also exhibited the Ferris wheel and the roller coaster, sights of wonder to nearly everyone, especially those who actually rode on these contraptions.

A TALENT TO AMUSE

It didn't take long for entrepreneurs to come up with a concept featuring exotic attractions in more permanent locations.

These were called amusement parks, and promoters began to build them near the seaside and lakes at the end of streetcar lines, thereby making them accessible to everyone, rich and poor alike. The best sections of the beach were set aside for the wealthy, while working-class families were often confined to beaches with rocks and sewage, and longer walks to the restrooms.

Before the World's Columbian Exposition even opened, the Atlantic City beach resort was competing for leisure-time revenue. Shortly before the Civil War, some Philadelphia businessmen had noticed an insect-plagued, wind-beaten, empty stretch of beach off the coast of New Jersey called Absecon Island. Through vision, good business sense, or dumb luck, the entrepreneurs viewed this unattractive island as a potential gold mine. They bought it, then persuaded the Camden and Atlantic Railroad to lay a railroad line from Philadelphia. Soon they began to lure customers with excursion fares and promises of clean air, an invigorating dip in the ocean, a cure for their aches and pains, and an opportunity to meet the man or woman of their dreams. If the potential customer already had a family, his children would adore him for taking them to this golden sash of sand for a few days of heaven. Or so the advertising said.

Once the Columbia Exposition gave the world a glimpse of the fun that could be experienced at an amusement park, Atlantic City's potential leapfrogged ahead. Quickly it captured the attention of those who'd just discovered the concept of leisure time. Residents of tenement housing in Philadelphia stuffed baskets full of sandwiches and warm beer before boarding railroad cars to escape the suffocating heat of summer. Known as day-trippers, these exhausted folks were released an hour and a half later from the confinement of the crowded railroad cars and rushed to join thousands of other vacationers for a day by the Jersey shore. They didn't want to miss a minute of their holiday by the sea. If they had swimming suits, they wore them. If they didn't, they wore their underwear or their outerwear, or sometimes nothing at all.

Hotels and boardinghouses quickly rose as true examples of cookie-cutter architecture, while greasy eating establishments popped up and gave everyone indigestion and gout. But the adventurous few arriving for a day or weekend away from the murky depths of nearby cities didn't complain. After all, this may have been the first vacation they'd ever had.

Cookie-cutter hotels (an inexpensive form of architecture that allowed buildings no individuality) were built at Atlantic City in the late 1800s to accommodate the rising numbers of vacationers.

But well-to-do people knew better and demanded finer accommodations. They didn't have long to wait. More hotels were built in Atlantic City; these soon charged nine dollars a day for room and board, although day-trippers couldn't afford this astronomical price. For this princely amount, the hotel provided such luxuries as a forty-piece orchestra that sere-naded residents at breakfast. In the afternoon, after an exhausting day of a short swim in the ocean and a long nap on the veranda, maids and butlers served full teas.

The maids and butlers were primarily African-American, as were many of the other laborers who had heard about the jobs available to them and arrived from the South with great expectations. Because the hotels were closed during the off season, they were without an income for a part of the year and suffered as a result. Little is known of how the hotel staff lived during these months, but few could afford to go south to their former homes. Much of the credit for Atlantic City's quick growth is given to the black labor force that came to town, hoping for better lives.

Atlantic City actually had beaches that were informally sectioned off to teenagers, senior citizens, and ethnic groups. The African-Americans had a beach called Chicken Bone Beach at the end of Missouri Avenue, where they gathered with friends and families to enjoy ocean breezes on hot summer days. Fortunately, beaches are no longer segregated at Atlantic City or anywhere else. Segregation officially ended when the Civil Rights Act was passed in 1964.

An African-American couple in swimwear, posing on the beach at Atlantic City, New Jersey; 1920s.

Following Atlantic City's example, millionaires elsewhere on the eastern seaboard demanded exclusive seaside resorts. Builders at such places as Bar Harbor, Maine; Marblehead, Massachusetts; and Newport, Rhode Island, promised to exclude the "excursionists," another name for day-trippers. Despite the fact that the first and main attraction had been a holiday by the sea, very little swimming was done at the more exclusive resorts. Lavish mansions that were built in these resort areas were the scenes of dances, coming out parties, teas, and card playing, the preferred amusements of the moment. The competition among leaders of high society to build the biggest and most expensive "cottages" at Newport grew beyond reason. Henry James, a noted author of the day, called the gilded palaces by the sea a "breeding ground for white elephants."

THE BOARDWALK

Those who came to Atlantic City looking for fun and those in business by the shore who wanted to create that amusement for a price came to the same conclusion: sand was a nuisance, and just plain dirty once it left the shore. It got in shoes, in clothes, in empty food baskets, on railroad car seats, and on hotel floors, and it clogged up the drains at home—if the homes had drains. Finally, in 1870, the city council decided to build a footwalk along a stretch of the oceanfront at Atlantic City. Dimensions were declared and the wooden walk was laid down each summer season, then taken up and stored during the winter months.

Coney Island's mile and a half long boardwalk closely resembled Atlantic City's; early 1940s.

Ten years later, the first footwalk had been trampled to wood chips and a new, larger one put in its place. Commercial enterprises were told to keep their distance of ten feet, while bathhouses were ordered to stay farther away. As businesses grew in number and size, they crept onto the footwalk, now called the boardwalk. So did many visitors, who not only walked but also stayed to look at members of the opposite sex. Soon the boardwalk became known as a questionable, even dangerous, place to linger because visitors tripped or fell off while engaged in the serious occupation of flirting.

Severe storms washed away the next couple of boardwalks at Atlantic City, and not until the beginning of the twentieth century was one finally built to last. Forty feet wide, the walk was slightly more than four miles in length and was bordered with a handrail so that strollers could ogle without a spill. With a few minor changes, it is the boardwalk that is sauntered upon today, nearly a hundred years later. It quickly replaced the ocean as the main attraction at Atlantic City. Walkers strolled to see and be seen, every business along the boardwalk clamored for the attention of those with a few pennies to spend, and, most important, the walk kept the sand out of everyone's shoes!

The Shelburne was one of many hotels lining the boardwalk in Atlantic City, New Jersey; late 1930s.

AN ELEPHANT IN MY EYE

Atlantic City soon attracted more than day-trippers, the elite who stayed in nice hotels, and families who came for the sun and water. The resort quickly set a speed record in the race to become the bizarre capital of the world. How? By allowing the goofiest attractions to crowd their way onto the boardwalk and compete for the money of the visitor. Snake charmers, the man with the iron jaws, and the "learned pigs" (they had been trained) were just three diversions that seemed almost normal compared to the other weirdos-by-the-sea. A flagpole sitter stayed on high for forty-nine days; a 300-pound man ate 146 clams in twenty minutes; the Flying Zachinis were shot out of a cannon. Animal acts such as high-diving horses leaped from forty-foot towers, and Professor Nelson's Boxing Cats actually wore boxing gloves.

"Elephant hotel affords grand view of surrounding country," stated the advertising used to lure real estate buyers to the beach. Lucy the elephant was built in 1881 by promoter James V. Lafferty.

Then there was Lucy. In 1881, James V. Lafferty began to build an elephant of wood and metal to be used as a promotion for land sales along the ocean. At completion, Lucy weighed ninety tons, stood sixty-five feet high, and was thirty-eight feet long. Henry James could have used his white elephant quote all over again, because that's what Lucy was, in every sense of the word. Tourists didn't know what else to do with her after they'd climbed up the spiral stairway encased in her legs and looked out the windows on her body. Neither did the owner. For a while she became a tavern, then a summer cottage. But, like many summer cottages, she was empty most of the year and slowly began to fall apart. It looked as if she was headed for the scrap heap when the state of New Jersey declared her a landmark and patched her up in 1966. Today, she works just fine as a museum.

PIER PRESSURE

Six giant piers once extended into the sea from the boardwalk. They were the Garden Pier, the Steel Pier, the Central Pier, the Hines Pier, the Million Dollar Pier, and the Young Pier. Since Atlantic City's early days, they have housed the stars of the entertainment business. However, the entertainment that occurred on these piers was different from what appeared on the boardwalk. The pier acts had a semblance of normalcy, of real theater, not just strangeness paraded before the public. But the pier acts also were geared to satisfy the capricious tastes of the millions who flocked there seeking entertainment and relaxation. H. J. Heinz, the 57 varieties pickles and ketchup man, enticed everyone to his pier by giving away free pickles. John Lake Young bought an old quay in 1891 and turned it into a showcase for dancers and actors. Dora Johnson introduced a dance called the cakewalk, and Sarah Bernhardt came from England to attract thespian-lovers. The Million Dollar Pier brought the magician Harry Houdini to disappear on its stage, and Theodore Roosevelt, who became president of the United States, gave a speech there to promote his newly formed Bull Moose party.

As these piers were built up and down the boardwalk, they quickly became the principal stages on which many international stars made their first major appearances in the United States. The Beatles played on the Steel Pier in the sixties, and The Rolling Stones rocked the house a decade later. The Miss America Beauty Pageant originated on the Steel Pier. Three of these piers are left. The Hines Pier was demolished by a hurricane in 1944; the Million Dollar and Young Piers disappeared in other violent storms.

Today, millions of visitors head for Atlantic City for many reasons besides surf and sun and sand. But those are still the best reasons to come.

CHAPTER THREE

From Bloomers to Bikinis: Decades of Swimwear Design

Going to the beach became the recreation of choice in nineteenth-century Great Britain, and the United States quickly copied the idea. This created a crisis, however. No one understood what kind of clothing should be worn, but people knew they must cover up. Displaying one's body just wasn't acceptable in the 1800s. Lacking any other ideas, people wore their street clothes, complete with hat and gloves.

UNDER WRAPS

To truly get wet, however, and enjoy even a small amount of exercise, beachgoers realized they must come out from under wraps. At one point women draped themselves from head to foot in a kind of flannel casing, and the following rhyme was soon repeated up and down the beach:

> The ladies dressed in flannel cases
> Show nothing but their hands and faces.

Women dressed fashionably for this occasion, well-corseted for a bumpy ride at Seabreeze, Daytona Beach, Florida; 1900s.

Real bathing suits that proper women elected to wear still resembled their street clothes. Made of about twelve yards of woolen material in dreary colors of gray, black, and dark tan, the average beach costume was not fun or pretty to wear. Large pantaloons or bloomers hung down under a thick, long-sleeved dress. The costume often grew heavier when it was adorned with frills and flounces, and, should the wearer dare to go into the water, it acted as a kind of anchor. It was definitely not designed to be wet. Thick black stockings were also worn, since legs were not to be bared in public. Bathing shoes didn't appear until 1893; they resembled ballet slippers.

Women tried to be fashionable at all costs. Corsets worn

underneath their bathing suits pinched in their waists, causing cramps and stomach upsets. Orson S. Fowler, an American phrenologist (someone who believes that a person's mental faculties are indicated by the shape of his or her skull), publicly stated that corsets caused hysteria and insanity in women who wore them. It didn't matter what anyone said, however. Women wore corsets under all their garments except their nightgowns. If a woman had stepped into the surf in this attire, she could easily have been dragged under by the sheer weight of her clothes alone. Swimming was not an option in this getup.

Men's bathing suits at this time looked much like their underwear, and that in itself shocked the faint of heart. To counteract this near-sinful sight on the beach, men added stripes to their pullovers and pants, thereby creating a convicts-at-play look. In the words of one observer, men looked like creatures "that the land is trying to shake off and the sea is unwilling to take."

This illustration is typical of those used for publications and postcards as the beach grew in popularity as a recreation destination; men added stripes to bathing suits so they wouldn't look like underwear (date unknown).

Postcards at the turn of the
century accurately depicted
beach fashions of the day as
well as the romantic mystique
surrounding the beach
experience.

Shortly after the turn of the century, bathing attire began to relax. Resort life at the seashore had developed, and people actually wanted to swim for exercise. Not only was a twenty-two-pound soggy bathing suit impossible for women to wear, but men didn't find it attractive.

Quickly, looks became as important as custom, and it was decided by popular acclaim that the sight of skin was not as much of a disgrace as it used to be. Short sleeves replaced long; pantaloons grew shorter to reveal ankles that could be seen through transparent silk stockings. But the old corset still remained under the new swimwear. So did the danger to a passerby of being snapped by untrustworthy corset supports, which were no longer held in place by layers and layers of clothing.

REBELLION IN THE RANKS

In 1905, the Sears, Roebuck and Co. catalog advertised only two swimming costumes for women. The skirts were long and now considered dangerous by the public, since they might interfere with actual movements in the water; the black stockings were heavy and hot; and the collar buttoned up around the throat in a kind of choke hold. The price for the complete outfit, including bloomers, came to $2.98. A bathing cap was thrown in for that price, and the catalog advertisement suggested it would also be useful around the house as a dust cap.

Although women's shapes were still described as "roBUST and HYPnotic," the winds of change rustled along the shores of the nation. Murmurs of dissent appeared in the fashion magazines. "A woman's clothing interferes much with the free play of muscles," one magazine writer stated. But women had forgotten one thing: Showing off more while wearing less would expose their shapes. Many felt the need to diet and exercise to go along with this dress change. Further, society hadn't completely approved. Yet women persevered and quickly decided they would rather be ostracized than corseted on the beach.

ALONG CAME ANNETTE

As women were reshaping themselves, they were demanding reshaped swimsuits. In 1907, one woman came to the rescue of all. She was an Australian named Annette Kellerman, who had contracted polio as a child and begun to swim to strengthen her leg muscles. Because she did not want to swim "wearing more stuff than I hang on a clothes line," she devised her own suit. It was a body stocking with the legs cut off two inches above the knees. When Kellerman first appeared at Boston's Revere Beach, she was arrested for indecent exposure. Yet women were speaking up about fashion in all areas of their lives, and changes continued to take place. Two years later, corsets had disappeared completely, and the Kellerman suit was in vogue at the seashore.

Five women in a typical pose of the late 1920s, seen on a Florida beach.

As the bathing suit and the wearer became more streamlined, both began to appear in newspaper and magazine advertising. While the new look sold real estate, especially in Florida, it continued to horrify officials who were resistant to change. Even with Annette Kellerman leading the way, public officials would not allow women on the beach at Atlantic City without stockings. Offenders would be punished to the full extent of the law. In 1913, when a woman wore a shortened version of the bathing suit, bathers at Atlantic City pelted her with "epithets and sand."

Examples of policing by public officials continued for many years and seemed to attract more attention than one of those new contraptions called *aeroplanes*. Bathing suit regulations were posted at every resort and seashore, spelling out what could and what could not be worn. Confusion reigned, since the list was long and complicated. Although swimmers tried to comply, sooner or later they'd make a mistake and be arrested. Not only that, but a bather could land in jail for indecent exposure should she outgrow last year's swimsuit and try to wear it anyway.

AN ERA ENDS AND ANOTHER BEGINS

At the end of World War I and the beginning of the twenties, women freed themselves from more restrictions. They got the vote, they cut their hair, and if skin was in, so was skinny. They lost their curves with their corsets and wore dresses that had no waists and barely covered their knees. Swimsuits followed fashion and grew shorter, baring women's upper arms and back as well.

Hollywood and big business conspired to free women's bathing suit fashions from the prevailing rules and regulations of postwar social culture. But it took a very small business at first to get things going. In 1910, Carl Jantzen and his partners, John and Roy Zehntbauer, operated a small knitting company in Portland, Oregon. They produced heavy wool sweaters as well as socks and gloves, which were knitted on hand-operated machines. They could have remained a small, obscure company if it hadn't been for a rowing club's request for swim trunks that would withstand chilly Oregon mornings.

The Mureen family on a fishing trip to Wisconsin stop for a swim in a nearby lake; 1926.

Intrigued by the challenge, the owners soon produced one-piece swimsuits from the same rib-stitch equipment used to make sweater cuffs.

Although these suits weighed eight pounds when wet, no one cared. Both men and women wore this early design, including the tasseled hat. Women gave in to the demands of society and added long black stockings to their costumes.

As more and more of these suits were seen on the beach, the effect on the American fashion public was electrifying. By 1928, the company had achieved worldwide distribution and, for many years, the public referred to these suits as Jantzens in honor of the man who designed them. Everyone who swam or sunned wanted the freedom and the look of a suit like the rib stitch. Other companies joined in the production of these suits, and an industry was born, advertising their products with the help of starlets from Hollywood.

In 1920, the Jantzen Company featured an outline of a diving girl wearing a red swimsuit in a catalog illustration. Soon after it appeared, a Jantzen store manager cut out several diving girls from the catalog and pasted them on the store window. Then a young man dropped by and asked for a dozen additional catalogs. He told the salesclerk that he had put the red diving girl on the windshield of his car and now

A child model in a Jantzen playsuit bearing the red diving-girl logo poses for a catalog illustration; 1931.

all his friends wanted to do the same. Soon the diving girl logo became an essential part of the Jantzen advertising campaign.

In 1923, company officials went to a convention in Washington, D.C., and took decals of the red diving girl with them. Word got around that Jantzen officials were giving out decals at each train stop along the way. In Billings, Montana, taxi drivers mobbed the train, and in Pittsburgh, Pennsylvania, motorists blocked streets leading to the train station and threatened to riot unless they received decals. By the time the train finally reached the nation's capital, it had been nicknamed "The Diving Girl Special." The red diving girl became America's first pinup, and she appeared on the windshields of more than four million cars. Police chiefs in Boston, Massachusetts; Rockford, Illinois; and other cities finally banned them "in the interests of public safety." The diving girl continues to represent the company even today, although she has changed to reflect the style changes in swimwear. The diving girl still reigns as the first swimsuit queen.

The stock market crash in 1929 caused economic chaos in the nation and more confusion about swimwear at the beach. To stimulate interest and sales during the Depression, novelty suits that no one could afford showed up in advertising

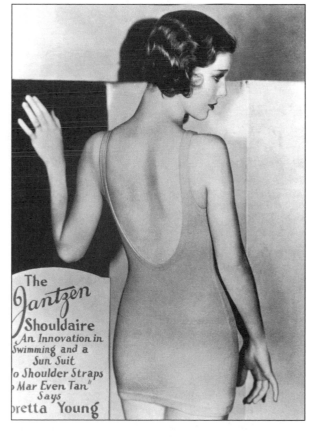

Popular movie star Loretta Young posed for the Jantzen Company to promote her career as well as the swimsuit; 1931.

and publicity stunts. Suits made of seaweed, wood fiber, or even rabbit fur were tried, perhaps to distract citizens from their financial problems.

As the Depression continued into the thirties, people went to the beaches in increasing numbers. It didn't cost anything, and the activities were different, sometimes bordering on strange. Baby pig races were conducted by women dressed in the latest swimsuits. Blocks of ice were carried by bathing beauties who then raced for the dubious honor of being first and becoming Ice-Block Race Queen. Even better, the bathing suits being designed at this time attempted to make everyone look like a movie star. In fact, many well-known stars of the day, including Loretta Young, Douglas Fairbanks Jr., and Dick Powell, appeared in advertisements that increased sales in these down times. Somehow people managed to find a few extra dollars for a new swimsuit. Sales figures tell us that twelve million suits were sold in 1931.

If women's suits were designed to show more of a well-developed figure, men's suits were not. The battle began to let men wear trunks only, but the beach police would not allow it. So the designers built in a top to the trunks that could be removed with a zipper when the censors removed the rules. Not until 1937 did men

While a featured actor for Warner Brothers, Dick Powell modeled Jantzen's "Topper" swimsuit; 1933.

ZIP—from Suit to Trunks

Jantzen

MOLDED-FIT
swimming suits

THE
TOPPER

DICK POWELL

overcome the backwash of censorship and win the right to go bare chested on public beaches.

SWIMSUITS GO TO WAR

As the thirties ended, the world inched closer to another war. After the United States entered World War II in 1941, it commandeered textile and manufacturing companies to make uniforms and weaponry. Production on swimsuits was severely curtailed, although designers were inspired by military fashion and fabrics to create a series of "camouflage" swimsuits for the beach replacing the bright hues once found

Betty Grable's swimsuit pictures were sent to millions of servicemen during World War II; 1941–1945.

there. Output was minimal, however, as people didn't mind using old suits, a small sacrifice for the war effort. Soldiers who requested photographs of their favorite movie personalities usually received one of the star posing in a swimsuit. Millions of photographs of Betty Grable in a swimsuit reached soldiers wherever they were stationed. Most companies like Jantzen made sleeping bags and sweaters for soldiers, while other swimsuit companies such as Cole of California made parachutes and tents. Lastex, the rubber-based foundation of many swimsuit designs, went to war as well. Once the war ended in 1945, the swimsuit industry plunged back into manufacturing, using new technology, textiles, and synthetics all developed for the military.

The following year, two French designers intro-

Interior scene of Jantzen factory shows workers sewing clothing for soldiers during the latter part of World War II; 1944.

duced a modified two-piece bathing suit that created a media sensation. French models were photographed on French sand wearing the design, which once again brought out the beach police in great numbers.

In that same year something else caused another kind of media sensation. The United States set off a series of atomic-bomb tests in a little-known place in the Pacific Ocean called the Bikini atoll. Since the French designers hadn't come up with a fitting name for their abbreviated bathing suit yet, they took the word that had been appearing in the news and called their suit the bikini.

Using less than a yard of material to make, the bikini caused as much of a commotion as the suits in Queen Victoria's time that required twelve yards of fabric in their construction. Public beaches banned the bikini for more than ten years, and many people in all walks of life found something to say about it—all bad. Fashion decided to return to more conventional swimsuits, and soon there was a cover-up at the beach once again.

GOING MOD WITH THE BOD

In the years since then, swimsuit fashion has changed nearly every decade, sometimes recycling old ideas with new fabrics before moving on to another style with a newly invented synthetic. Even corsets made a comeback in the fifties, when padding and wires were employed as aids for women who were not satisfied with the way they looked.

The sixties developed into a rebellious decade when young people wanted to change everything, especially what they wore to the beach. New fabrics such as Lycra, a commercial name for spandex, allowed the "less is more" philosophy to take over. Two-piece suits became the uniform of the day, as the bikini recycled to the accompaniment of songs such as "Itsy-Bitsy Teenie Weenie Yellow Polka Dot Bikini" and the rush of beach movies starring Annette Funicello and Frankie Avalon. (Eventually, more than a hundred beach movies would be filmed before the decade ended.) Even Barbie and Ken dolls wore swimsuits. It was a decade dedicated to the youth of the nation whose life's work seemed to be found only at the beach.

The seventies saw a continued emphasis on experimental designs made of metallic materials as well as briefer suits: top-

Esther Williams starred in many swimming movies during the 1940s and 1950s, and posed in swimsuits to promote them.

Jantzen began to promote health as well as beauty in their advertising illustrations; 1940s.

less suits for women, Speedos for men, and thongs for everyone. As swimsuits for men and women continued to disappear by the ounce and more and more of their bodies went on display, it slowly became apparent that something else was required to look good at the beach. However, some effort on the part of the beachgoer would be needed.

Serious health buffs and bodybuilders had been exercising and following healthful diets for a long time; now these habits became a part of the overall picture. Practicing good nutrition and exercise gave everyone an opportunity to look their best. Swimming for competition as well as exercise brought about a resurgence of the 1920s tank suit. It grew in popularity during the 1980s, reflecting the healthy attitude that has prevailed into the twenty-first century.

CHAPTER FOUR

Beach Blanket Bingo: Things to Do at the Beach

What is there to do at the beach? A few rules specifying safety and good taste should always be observed. But after that, almost anything goes. Over the years, vacationers have thought of highly creative things to do while there. Believe it or not, at one time a bathing beauty contest was thought to be not only daring but a very original idea.

BATHING BEAUTY CONTESTS . . .
BY THE BEAUTIFUL BEACH

It's been said that beauty is only skin deep, although it took a while for many folks to reveal enough to be judged. The Greeks decorated their public baths with mosaics of bathing beauties, parading their curves for all to admire. But Greek women seldom appeared in public in bathing attire, so there was little chance to judge who was fairest among them. Leave it to Americans for turning beauty into a contest. When a few local promoters cast about for an event that would help popularize Atlantic City, they decided to concentrate on who looked best in a bathing suit.

The problem was simple, really. After Labor Day, everyone went home and forgot about the beach. But the sun still shone, the waves continued to roll in, there was life after Labor Day—just no customers. Quite possibly one more week of revenue could be squeezed out of the public if there was an activity to keep them there or bring them back to the shore. The Atlantic City promoters quickly organized a fall pageant that would feature such attractions as a rolling chair parade, a night spectacle, and a bathers' revue. Entries were sought for all events, the only requirement being that everyone, even in the rolling chair parade, had to look good in a bathing suit. Out of all this concentration on bathing suits the Inner-City Beauty Contest was born.

The first contest in 1921 featured seven entrants and became the hit of the fall pageant, attracting a crowd as well as plenty of newspaper reporters to spread the word. Not quite sixteen, Margaret Gorman was crowned the first Miss America, and her sweet, innocent demeanor quieted any would-be critics about a worldly event that placed emphasis on female figures. But not for long. Within a short time, the skin police complained that innocent young girls' heads could be filled with "vicious" ideas if this parade of beauties were allowed to continue. The *New York Times* declared that it was a "reprehensible way to advertise Atlantic City."

The promoters, not wanting to give up this well-attended event, paid particular attention to the critics and saw to it that each Miss America reflected the most innocent and pure ideals of the land. Miss America of 1927, Lois Delandor, seemed to be such a person. She had unbobbed hair, did not smoke or eat pickles (not allowed for contestants), and won her crown on her parents' twentieth wedding anniversary. But nothing helped win over the critics, not even refraining from pickles. After the following year the city abandoned the contest because of its tarnished reputation, not to be revived until 1935.

Lois Delandor, Miss America of 1927, strikes a queenly pose in her celebration photograph.

A number of changes were made in the years to come. Contestants had to have more than a pretty face and figure. They now had to demonstrate a talent as well, exhibit some congeniality, and wear something else besides just a bathing suit. In 1940, the event moved to the Convention Center in Atlantic City, where it has remained since and become an American institution. By 1995, the seventy-fifth anniversary of the Miss America Pageant, more than $100 million in educational grants had been awarded, making the organization the largest provider of scholarships for women in the world. Margaret Gorman would have been amazed. She received nothing except a sash, a lopsided crown, and the honor of being the first Miss America.

BUILDING SAND CASTLES A GRAIN AT A TIME

No one knows who built the very first sand castle or sculpture. But evidence has been found to show that ancient Egyptians

Sand sculptures on the beach at Atlantic City, New Jersey; late 1930s.

built sand sculptures some four thousand years ago. Naturally, they created replicas of pyramids and monuments, since castles hadn't yet been invented. Americans got caught up in sand sculpting in the 1800s. Philip McCord is given credit for being the earliest sand artist who worked alongside the Atlantic City boardwalk in 1897. He set himself up in business to sculpt interesting scenes made entirely of sand, and he lived on the donations of beach visitors passing by.

McCord was joined by other carvers who quickly crowded the beaches with sandy portraits of prominent people of the day. President Woodrow Wilson was a favorite. Later, so was the aviator Charles Lindbergh. They also depicted prominent works of art, such as Washington crossing the Delaware and the Crucifixion. King Neptune seated on a seashell throne became another popular candidate for grainy posterity. Storms were not considerate of the sand sculptors, however, and washed away their masterpieces. The artists added cement to their mixes, but that didn't help when the hurricane of 1944 sandbagged their work entirely, and the city council told the carvers to pack up and move elsewhere.

Contests for sand castling actually began in 1952 in Fort Lauderdale, Florida, at a Fourth of July festival. West Coast venues were soon added, contributing to the popularity of the activity. Sand castling seems to have an affinity for natural disasters. In 1964, a tsunami caused by the Alaskan earthquake destroyed a bridge connecting the town of Cannon Beach, Oregon, to the rest of the state. This forced the residents to think of an event that would keep their children entertained during the rebuilding of the bridge, so they decided to try a sand castle contest. It was so successful that the town continued

This 1950s postcard of Jacksonville Beach, Florida, testifies to the growing popularity of sand castle building.

A sand castle built for the Cannon Beach, Oregon, contest; July 1992.

the event for the tourists who visited after the state reconstructed the bridge.

Now, each June, thousands of people come to watch or build sand castles. From sand dabblers to competitive teams, everyone shares in the fun. The rules are simple. No themes for the creations; each contestant or team is simply given a plot of sand as a space on which to build. Sand may not be added or removed, and only natural materials such as seaweed, shells, or rocks may be used for ornamentation. Today, the Cannon Beach contest is one of the largest sand sculpting events in the West.

It isn't difficult to build a sand castle. The ingredients are right on the beach: sand and water. Seawater is a good bonding agent, because the salt crystals will form a crust over the surface of the sculpture. The best location for the sandy creation is just above the high tide line. Simple tools are preferred: shovels, trowels, pails, and containers into which sand can be packed and formed into shapes.

A WORLD OF SAND

Not everyone is as curious about sand as the members of the International Sand Collectors Society (ISCS), whose fascination for it is hard to beat. They make the point that sand is one of the most common substances on earth, so common that people don't really give it the attention it deserves. And we should.

Sand cushions our land against the ocean's impact. It's an important construction material, and a necessary component in the production of concrete and glass. It gets between our toes on every beach we walk on, and what playground doesn't have sand under the swing sets to soften a child's fall?

This type of sand (magnified ten times), called foraminifera, has grains about one millimeter in diameter. It was found near Sanur, Bali.

Collectors enjoy identifying the sand they collect. There are six classes of roundness and many classifications of size. Most everyone knows the difference between a granule and a boulder, but how many know what ooid sand is? And has anyone seen black or green or red sand? Here's a hint: green sand is found at Green Sand Beach on the Big Island of Hawaii.

Sand travels, as everyone knows, transported by wind, ocean currents, and waves. Sand that is blowing with the wind will often pile up around obstacles, such as boulders and bushes. These pileups, called sand dunes, can be as small as a few feet to fifty or even a hundred feet high. Some of these dunes have acoustic properties and are also known as singing or barking sand. They boom, roar, or bark, depending on who is listening to identify the sound. A physicist member of the ISCS claims that most booming sand occurs in the desert, while singing or squeaking sand occurs along beaches and lakeshores. Two examples of American beaches possessing this unique acoustical quality are Barking Sands Beach on Kauai, Hawaii, and Singing Sand Beach near Marblehead, Massachusetts. Dragging your bare feet on the dry sand will cause it to "sing" or make a humming sound.

MUSCLING IN AT MUSCLE BEACH

Just a few steps from the pier on the beach at Santa Monica, California, there's a plaque that reads "The Original Location of Muscle Beach. The Birthplace of the Physical Fitness Boom of the Twentieth Century." The physical fitness craze probably began here, although no one can agree exactly when. Some say that in the mid-thirties a playground instructor installed parallel bars, rings, and a tumbling platform for the kids who came to the beach. Chess and checkers were added for those who wanted to exercise their minds.

But no one was thinking about muscles then. Strong young kids used the bars and the rings to toss themselves around in the air, and used each other for handstanding, pyramids, and flip-flops. That area of sand quickly became known as an outdoor gymnasium where muscular boys and girls could learn, perform, and teach others how to do the same thing.

Les and Pudgy Stockton handstanding at Muscle Beach, Venice, California, with two other performers; early 1940s.

They began to lift weights at the beach to grow even stronger and also to improve the look of their bodies. Soon these weightlifters had earned a reputation for being totally weird.

Before long, a group of men and a few women worked out at the beach every day at the same time and in the same place. People began to show up just to watch. Then the recreation department asked if the weightlifters and acrobats would consider being regular summer acts. When thousands of people came to see them perform, Muscle Beach was born big-time.

Although there were many kings of Muscle Beach, Abby Eville Stockton was the undisputed queen. Born in 1917, she grew up along the beaches of California, nicknamed Pudgy not because she was plump but because her family found her so determined. She is now in her eighties, and the nickname still sticks. In the beginning she thought that only men should have muscles until she met Les Stockton. He was a member of the UCLA gymnastics team and persuaded Pudgy to lift a few barbells and learn handstands, thereby spending more time with him on the beach. Soon they were a romantic couple and also summer acrobats and weightlifters with the other regulars at Muscle Beach. Often they partnered in acrobatic shows, with tiny 110-pound Pudgy holding 180-pound Les in a handstand. When Les joined what is now the Air Force during World War II, they married, and Pudgy followed him to his camp assignments, managing to work out and teach other women how to become exercise enthusiasts as well. She was always careful to say that it was for maintaining body weight

Pudgy Stockton lifting a handstanding friend at Muscle Beach, Venice, California; early 1940s.

Pudgy Stockton exercises at Muscle Beach, Venice, California; early 1940s.

only, never to build bodies that displayed muscles. The world wasn't yet ready for that in women.

After the war, Pudgy opened a gym for women, the first in the country, while Les ran one for men. "I got such a feeling of confidence from what I could do with my body," Pudgy said. "I wanted others to have that same feeling." Quite clearly she helped give physical fitness a dramatic importance to many women's lives.

A modern Muscle Beach exists today in Venice, a seaside community just outside of Los Angeles. Attention is focused on the "Pit," cordoned off for the serious bodybuilders. It's an area filled with weightlifting equipment. Spectators wait along the boardwalk to see the giants of physical fitness practice their routines and fine-tune their muscles. Who knows? Maybe one day they'll become wrestlers or even governors. Today's Muscle Beach spawns more than just another pretty pec.

WHEN CALORIES DON'T COUNT

Food is a vital part of going to the beach. A stroll, an afternoon, a day at the beach brings out an appetite in everyone. People fill coolers and baskets full of favorite food for every member of the family. Fantastic picnics are packed to impress the new boyfriend or girlfriend, cookouts on fire pits planned for family reunions, health foods carried for the athletes. And the ven-

In the late 1880s, Joseph Fralinger was among the first to open a store that made and served food and candy for beachgoers.

dors! The boardwalks are lined with every hot dog, ice cream, cotton candy, and sandwich salesman ready and willing to hand over a bunch of calories for a not-so-modest sum.

In the early years of beachgoing, vacationers packed their own picnics, but that didn't last long. Joseph Fralinger was among the first to get the idea that folks might want something to eat at the beach that was not of their own making. Early in Atlantic City history, he sold cider, apples, and lemonade, even juggling lemons to get the attention of passersby. Then he set up candy and fruit stands, too. Although Fralinger may have sold the first taffy, David Bradley gets the credit for inventing the name. One night in 1883, his candy stand was swamped by a storm. Not one to take a direct hit from adversity, the next day he decided to call his candy saltwater taffy. Although the taffy's been dry ever since, the name has stuck.

Nathan Handwerker came to Coney Island in 1915 and soon began selling hot dogs in a building at Surf and Stillwell Avenues. Although there were fancier places to eat, customers became convinced that a nickel was well spent at Nathan's. Forty years later, on July 6, 1955, he sold his hundred millionth hot dog.

Hot dogs, one of the most popular foods at Coney Island, cost a nickel in the early days. Now they cost at least two dollars and are simply referred to as hots, but they remain a favorite, with hot dog eating contests taking place every Fourth of July. The world's record is held by Kazutoyo "The Rabbit" Arai, a visitor from Japan. On July Fourth, 2000, he gulped down 25⅛ hot dogs in twelve minutes at Coney Island.

Now, the ultimate beach recipe:

> *Spaghettini with Sand*
> 1 pound spaghettini, or thin spaghetti
> ¼ cup olive oil
> 2 cloves garlic (peeled and crushed)
> ⅛ teaspoon crushed red pepper flakes
> ½ cup medium-coarse sand grains

(If you prefer a more crunchy texture, use quartz; if you want a more colorful and festive dish, use a combination of quartz, garnet, and olivine. Optional: 1 cup fresh bread crumbs can be substituted for sand.) Bring a large pot of water with a pinch of salt to boil. Add pasta and cook until tender. Heat a large frying pan and add the oil, garlic, and red pepper flakes; sauté a few seconds, but do not burn. Drain pasta and add it along with the sand (or bread crumbs) to the pan. Add salt and toss until the pasta is coated. Garnish with chopped parsley and grated cheese.

(While it may seem like a joke, this recipe is very real among sand collectors.)

And then there are those glorious cookouts for breakfast, lunch, and dinner. From clambakes on Cape Cod to luaus on Lanai or fish fries on the Mississippi River, calories don't really count. Coconuts tapped for their delicacies, snow cones, and frozen bananas were just a few of the favorite treats that drew great expectations from the boardwalk revelers. The food experience reflects one of the most entertaining pastimes and reasons people go to the beach. Some beachgoers can't decide whether to sit closer to the waves or the hot dog stand.

Breakfast cookouts, such as this one on a Lake Michigan beach near Frankfort, Michigan, are popular activities; 1980.

CHAPTER FIVE

The Ultimate Rush: Sports for Surf and Sand

There are two kinds of people who go to the beach: those who move and those who don't. The ones who don't move should pay special attention to this chapter. Getting in on the action just might be catching.

GO FLY A KITE

Kites most likely originated in China more than two thousand years ago. During that time they've had many functions. In the United States, Benjamin Franklin used a kite for his experiments with electricity during a thunderstorm. The Wright Brothers converted a kite into a glider, then into a powered airplane. From 1893 to 1933, the National Weather Service operated kite stations to measure humidity, temperature, and barometric pressure at different elevations and wind speeds.

The best use of kites, however, has been for entertainment. Every spring thousands of kites catch the wind from backyards, fields, parks, and beaches. But kites aren't your average newspaper, stick, and string construction anymore. Now kite builders use the latest technology and modern materials including nylon, fiberglass, plastics, and braided synthetics. Kites can range from postage stamp size to giants with hundreds of square feet of surface. The new materials allow contemporary and traditional styles to be flown by one person or a team of fliers in competition. That's right, kite flying is now a team sport, and the best place to fly is at the beach.

Kite flying at the beach is a favorite occupation of many beachgoers; Cannon Beach, Oregon, festival, mid-1990s.

SURFING THE ULTIMATE WAVE

Gnarly. Grommet. Barney. Alley-oop. Wipe out. Clueless about the meaning of these words? A duck-diving goofy-foot who goes all out for the macker, ripping into a tube and enjoying a visit to the green room, gets it. "Stoked" barely describes the rush. But you'd have to be a surfer to understand any of the above.

It's a different world, this surfing. Different words, different clothes, a different state of mind and being. Fishermen, probably in Polynesia, started the sport although that's not what they intended. They had to get their small crafts on the other side of the surf in order to bring in a day's catch so they could feed their families. British explorer Captain James Cook happened to notice these fishermen surfing to their boats and reported it as early as 1777 at Matavai Point in Tahiti. When he arrived in Hawaii the following year, he discovered fishermen there who were also surfing to their boats for the same reason.

Missionaries considered this activity immoral, probably because the men weren't fully clothed, and nearly eliminated it from island life. But the activity refused to go away. In 1907, George Freeth demonstrated surfing while visiting California from Hawaii. An Olympic swimmer, Duke Paoa Kahana-moku popularized it a few years later when he, too, traveled to California and put on surfing demonstrations.

Surfing was only for the strong and fit in the early days when the boards weighed 150 pounds. Lightweight balsa boards were introduced in the forties and polyurethane foam boards in the fifties. Surfing changed forever then, as lighter and less expensive boards made the sport accessible to every-one. In the sixties a string of beach movies confirmed surfing's position as a favorite water sport. Surf music, such as "Surfin'," "Surfer Moon," and "Catch a Wave" sung by the Beach Boys, and movies, such as *Where the Boys Are, Muscle Beach Party,* and *How to Stuff a Wild Bikini,* helped turn surfing into a national craze. After the invention of snug-fitting neoprene rubber wetsuits, surfing became a year-round sport.

Professional surfing was introduced in the late seventies. By the following decade, surf fashion had become a $2-billion-a-year industry while board weights had shrunk to eight pounds. Some surfers found jobs that paid a decent wage and were able to support their families.

P. J. Wahl is one of the lucky ones. He wanted to continue surfing just for the fun of it, but he needed to support his wife and five children. So he became a shaper, turning blanks of polyurethane into beautifully crafted surfboards before sending them off to be resined and sold in stores. Each piece is a work of art, taking him from three to four hours to refine. He works in a room painted black with lighting placed at a special height to show him the emerging profile of his work.

P. J. begins with a handsaw, cutting the "blank," or rectangular piece of polyurethane foam, into a rough shape resembling a surfboard. Each blank has a narrow piece of wood called a stringer down the center, to provide strength to the board. Then P. J. sands, turning the piece in progress around and around, angling it just so until he is satisfied that the shape and the edges, or rails, are perfect. Sometimes he works with lights on; sometimes they are dimmed so that he can catch each nuance of the "rocker," or slightly curved surface. It's almost as if he's shaping the board to fit the sea.

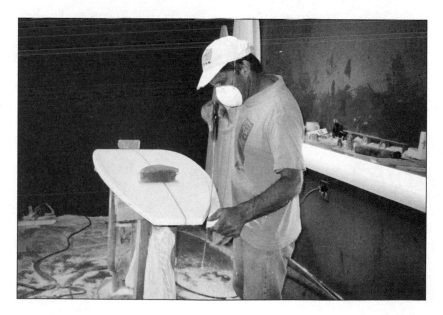

P. J. Wahl, of Pismo Beach, California, shapes surfboards in his studio behind his home; 1999.

In Hawaii, children always learn to surf with an adult. Waikiki is a good beginner's site. Teacher and student paddle out to where the waves are just barely breaking. They sit on their boards until they see a wave coming in. Then they turn their boards toward the beach. As the waves reach them, the teacher gives the student a push and yells, "Stand up." In an instant the student is up and riding toward shore.

John Clark at the age of ten, shown with his ten-foot balsa surfboard in Oahu, Hawaii; 1956.

John Clark is a writer, surfer, and firefighter who has lived in Hawaii all his life. He says, "That's exactly how I learned how to surf when I was eight years old in 1954. And that is how I've taught hundreds of other children to surf since then. Before you go surfing though, you have to learn how to swim. While it's true that you'll have a leash around your ankle that secures you to your board, a wave will still toss you around when you wipe out, and you'll need to know what to do. And sometimes leashes break. When this happens, the waves will carry your board into the beach, and you'll have to swim all the way in to get it.

"Children in Hawaii are taken to the beach at an early age, so they get used to being around waves. Many island children have bodyboards that get them started riding waves close to shore. It's a good headstart program for board surfing. Some people like to catch waves without any kind of a board at all. That's called bodysurfing, and all you need is a pair of fins.

"After all these years I still surf regularly," says John Clark. "It's a great activity for physical exercise, it's an individual sport that you don't need a whole team to do, and it's free. The waves don't cost a thing."

SLAMS AND SPIKES, HAMMERS AND DINKS

Beach volleyball began in the twenties along the pier in Santa Monica, California, invented, probably, by people who hated to wear shoes while playing games. Hard court volleyball had been around since 1895 and was played at colleges for the most part. Popular with servicemen in both world wars, it became an Olympic sport in 1964. After that, it caught on with young people who wanted something more active to do at the beach, yet at the same time to stay dry and work on their tans.

Volleyball action shot on an unidentified beach; 1999.

Most competitors play for recreational reasons; however, some yearn to proceed to organized tournaments that lead to professional games. Whatever the reason for playing, it's necessary to speak the speak of volley girls and boys to get along. Wraparound Killer Loops and Billabong shorts aren't enough; the player has to sound the part as well as look it. For starters, a facial is a spike to the face. A "facial disgracial" is an extreme facial that sends a player out of the game. A dink is a ball that's played just over the net. Hammer is a downward hit and a lollipop is an easy serve. A volley dolly? A girl who likes to watch guys playing volleyball.

KAYAK KRUISING

Grandpa's generation probably wanted kayaks when they were kids, because they'd seen all those movie serials in the thirties about the Royal Canadian Mounted Police searching for dogs and boys in the Yukon. By the end of the movie, the mounties shed their red jackets and began to paddle up and down rivers in kayaks, searching for the little rascals. Usually the dogs rescued the mounties, but it was the kayak that was best remembered.

Kayaks have been around for eons, probably starting as early as 7000 B.C. It is well recorded that when Aleuts settled on islands near the Bering Straits, they paddled kayak-like boats to pass through rough seas and treacherous currents. Skeletal remains of the Aleuts show huge arm bones, indicating that their arms were well developed compared to the rest of their bodies. Since then, kayaks have been associated with unforgiving waters, propelled by arctic giants of the north.

Kayaking only looks hard, so they say. A young person can usually paddle around

Kayaking is one of the many action water sports enjoyed near Pismo Beach, California; 1999.

after just a few hours of instruction and supervision because the boat is so lightweight and stable. Today's models are sleekly made plastic boats, designed to handle ocean waves or whitewater rivers with ease.

Kayakers do not sit in their boats; they wear them. The boat must fit the paddlers so that they feel comfortable and snug as they ride. A spray skirt prevents them from becoming soaked by an overzealous wave, making both boats and paddlers watertight. From then on, paddlers and boats learn how to get along together.

When preparing to launch the kayak from the beach, the paddlers need to study the waves as if they were surfers. Surf waves arrive in sets, with lulls separating those sets. The paddlers time their charges into the ocean to catch the lulls. Once in a while the only way to go is by punching the waves, or spearing right through them. Maybe that's the most thrilling of all. Suitable advice for launching and landing a kayak is to pick a beach that looks accommodating. Guidebooks can be helpful and so can local tourist information centers. Perhaps the best thing to do is to follow a car that has a kayak tied to its roof to a water site. This may tell you everything you really need to know about finding local kayaking venues.

FRISBEE DOGS

Back in the 1970s a man named Alex Stein crashed a Los Angeles Dodgers baseball game with his Frisbee dog, Ashley Whippet, and performed a high-flying demonstration in front of a grandstand audience. It was also seen on nationwide television. Everyone loved it and the sport of canine Frisbee was born. Since then Disc Dog Clubs have leaped up all over the country. There are mailing lists, training schedules, special events, and even Web sites.

Ocean Beach is one of four dog beaches in San Diego County, California, where dogs may roam freely without a leash and play with their owners. Rules of behavior must be observed so that all visitors enjoy a happy stroll.

Some tips for dog owners to remember: Riptide and surf warnings apply to canines as well as to humans. Dogs' skin can sunburn, especially short-haired dogs, so don't forget sunblock. If your dog gets overheated, slow it down for a snooze under a beach umbrella. Before heading home, check your critter for cuts from shells or rocks and clean any abrasions. At home, soak its sore feet in cool water and give your friend more water to drink. Then it's time to let your dog kick back and get ready for the next Frisbee day.

Dogs playing along the beach.

THE ONE THAT GOT AWAY

There are many places to catch fish and several ways to catch them. Standing on the beach and casting into the surf is one well-known way; fishing from a pier or bridge or dock is another. Piers can be great places to get good fishing results. According to expert Spence Petros, fish are more attracted to wooden piers than to metal ones, and structures that extend farther out into the water are better than shorter piers or docks. Piers built lower to the water usually pay off simply because they provide more shade for the fish.

The Pensacola Bay Fishing Bridge in Pensacola, Florida, is a mile and a half long and offers drive-on fishing. Powerful lights under the bridge make night fishing exciting. If that sounds like overkill, there are more than eight hundred piers around the country that can probably provide the exact fishing conditions anyone could want. California alone has more than ninety-two piers. Charter boats specialize in big game fish, from tuna to wahoo, using light tackle casting, trolling, or live bait. However, kids with a bobber and a bent pin will probably have just as much fun standing on the beach by the ocean or lake.

The pier at Huntington Beach, California, attracts fishermen and strollers as well as photographers; 1999.

Back in the thirties, Stuart Silver was typical of young boys who spent summers on the beach. After school ended for the year, Stuart's father drove his family to the beach at Crystal Cove near Oceanside, California, where they parked their car and trailer. All summer long Stuart and his brother swam and fished in the surf, usually catching softshell crabs that their father used for bait. During World War II, the family needed a special permit to camp because of their proximity to a Marine Corps base. Stuart said that camping on the beach was an idyllic way to grow up.

The opportunity to go fishing is not an option for all boys and girls, so kid-friendly organizations, such as the Police Activities League, have stepped in to make that experience available for those who want to try it. Officers and other volunteers take boys and girls to nearby lakes, show them how to bait hooks and cast and reel, then step back to watch these young fishermen experience their first catch. Many of the fish

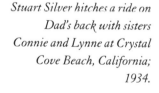

Stuart Silver hitches a ride on Dad's back with sisters Connie and Lynne at Crystal Cove Beach, California; 1934.

are throw backs; if the boys and girls want to keep their catch, the next lesson begins in cleaning. It may just be the beginning of a lifetime hobby, or a one-time experience.

TRY THEM ALL

Windsurfing is a young sport; its origins trace to the garages of two southern Californians named Jim Drake and Hoyle Schweitzer. Jim was a sailor and Hoyle a surfer; by 1968, they had morphed their two sports into one. Naturally, they called it windsurfing. They patented their sailboard, which they named Windsurfer, and soon they were in the business of making them. Simply put, they had mounted a sail on a universal joint. This required the sailor to support the rig, which could be tilted in any direction and steered without the use of a rudder.

Windsurfing is a common sport off the beaches of the Atlantic and Pacific; 1999.

By the late 1970s windsurfing had become a major phenomenon in Europe, and it soon caught on in the United States. The decade of the 1980s saw tremendous growth in the sport in America, with the birth of a World Cup tour and Olympic status in 1984. Equipment has developed concurrently until the board is highly specialized today, matching the skills of every age and ability.

Schools and equipment are available at most major windsurfing beaches. A list of the ten top beaches for this sport (see the end of this book) will give you a start on where to go; however, many other beaches offer equal opportunities to learn and enjoy.

Sailing, parasailing, waterskiing, snorkeling, scuba diving, boating, boogey boarding, bird watching, and water biking are a few more of the sports available at most beaches. The list grows longer every day. Can't decide what to do? Take a moment to mull over your interests, your talents, and your physical abilities before you decide. Counting waves may be the best sport of all.

CHAPTER SIX

Beach Equipment:
Once Upon a Pail and Shovel

People don't go to the beach without bringing half of every-thing they own. Towels, blankets, sun hats, visors, sunglasses, lotion, something to drink, something to eat, a cooler, a book, sunblock, sand pails, shovels, sand sifters, chair backs, sandals, a radio; has anything been overlooked? Sports equipment, of course, but that's another chapter. Let's take a look at some of the equipment that's cluttered the beaches of civilization for years.

A child on a beach near Richmond, Virginia, enjoys playing with a sand pail; circa 1935.

THE BATHING MACHINE

In the eighteenth century when "strip and plunge" became popular for therapeutic reasons in England, a bathing machine was needed in which one could change clothes, enter the water, and then be sub-merged by a person known as a dipper. A small wooden hut with doors on each end, sat atop a plat-form on wheels, and a horse in harness was needed to

pull the contraption into the water. When the bather inside was ready, a driver nudged the horse into action and it pulled the hut into the waves. Then the driver unfurled an awning over the door and unfolded some steps leading into the water. The bather descended and waited to be plunged into the cold sea again and again. The awning prevented the bather from being seen by others on the beach; therefore beachgoers soon labeled it a "modesty hood." These bathing machines remained popular as long as people were convinced that this dip into the icy cold waters restored their health or kept them strong and vigorous. Rows of the small houses on wheels, with horses patiently waiting to pull them back in, were a common sight at many English beaches until swimming as a sport replaced strip and plunge. Presumably the horses that stood in cold seawater all day were the healthiest in the kingdom.

It wouldn't be hard to come to the conclusion that some of the strip and plunge bathers would try to get away from the torturous experience, and swimming would be the most logical form of escape. One problem, though: not too many bathers knew how to swim. But the nonswimmers didn't have long to wait. Enterprising inventors soon would come to their aid with creative, if questionable, devices.

WEBS AND WINGS

Swimming as a sport was slow to catch on until 1587, when Everard Digby of England authored the first book that told readers how to swim. (He was a scholarly professor who wrote in Latin, not exactly the athletic type who wrote from experience.) Digby began his book by saying "one ought to swim both on the front and the back." Then he explained how to enter the water, how to swim on the front using breaststrokes and on the back using backstrokes. He mentioned no lifesaving skills or social or competitive reasons to swim. Digby wrote his book primarily to prevent accidents and drowning.

Interest in swimming grew as the global expansion of trade grew. English seamen on trading ships traveled the world and saw natives swim to their ships in tropical waters. They also observed workers in other countries who could swim underwater to repair ships. These swimmers looked to be in peak physical condition. The seamen came home and spread the word. Now there were more reasons to learn to swim: health and exercise.

In the nineteenth century, as swimming evolved into an athletic activity, men were encouraged to use mechanical appliances to help them learn the various strokes. Instruction books were soon published to teach them. Women were not even acknowledged in print as participants. Public opinion had long claimed that women were afraid of the water and therefore did not need to be included. The instruction books from that period show only men in sketches and later in photographs. Women were nowhere to be found, except on the beaches wearing their newfangled bathing clothes.

Air bladders, buoys, and floats were the first "tools" used. Soon fancy fins were sketched and patented, then actually tried. Webbed gloves or fins were slipped on hands and attached to the body by belts on the shoulders and around the wrists. A problem existed, however: the hands were held in such an unnatural splayed position in these contraptions that they soon cramped. In addition, the swimmer made no progress in the water because no one, except maybe a contortionist, could hold his hands in that position and still swim.

So the inventors next attacked the feet and legs of the swimmer. Flaps attached to legs proved to be of no use to the wearer. Wings attached to feet supposedly spread out behind the swimmer as he moved, to provide locomotion in the water. But they had little or no effect, probably because they must have been uncomfortable and slowed the swimmer due to the steel bands connected to his ankles.

Inventors tried other schemes: belts around the waist, and capes that looked like football players' shoulder pads extended to the swimmer's neck and face, complete with a kind of mask that fit over the mouth. Dunlop plates (named for the inventor) were offered to the public in 1875. They were flat surfaces of wood, attached to the hands and feet in order to provide more area of water to displace as the person swam. Dunlop plates gave little encouragement to swimmers wishing to break speed records.

Finally there were teachers' poles. A swimming teacher attached a stout wire to his student on a beltlike contraption. The wire was then fastened to a pole. The prospective swimmer entered the water, then the teacher pulled him along, leaving the student's arms free to stroke. He could be raised or lowered at the whim of the instructor, sort of like a mackerel dangling on the end of a fishing pole.

FARMERS TO THE RESCUE

In the mid-nineteenth century, farmers who lived near beaches also came to the aid of people learning to swim. On summer mornings farmers rattled up in huge wagons that they backed into the sea. Tying a strong rope to their wagons, they bravely waded out into the waves with the rope pulled taut behind them. Then bathers, hanging tightly to the rope, kicked and screamed with delight. Eventually, a creative carpenter built platforms with steps attached so that swimmers could climb onto the platforms, then dive from the top of the steps into the ocean. Today, at most beaches, those diving platforms are called rafts.

ROLLING CHAIRS

After Atlantic City became popular during the nineteenth century, visitors crowded the boardwalk to stroll and look at the many beach attractions. Invalids who came to the shore for

Rolling chairs on the boardwalk of Atlantic City, New Jersey; 1930s.

their health were not strong enough or able to walk. An enterprising hardware store operator bought some chairs with wheels attached to rent to visitors who couldn't walk. Called citadels of restful travel, they were soon as popular with those who were able to walk as those who were not. Then someone built rolling chairs for two or three occupants, and soon they were everywhere on the boardwalk, vying for space with foot travelers. Because of their numbers, the chairs were banned for a while but rolled back into favor with everyone in a few years, becoming mechanized in the forties and gradually diminishing in number in the fifties and sixties.

PAILS AND SHOVELS

Toys were originally castoffs from parents' tools or whatever could be found outdoors. In prehistoric times, children, sitting on the earthen floor by a fire, may have played with a bone that had been used to stir soup in a gourd. The first ball might have been a round stone. As civilization moved on, children played with containers, shovels, cups, plates—whatever came to hand and mind.

During frontier days in the United States, settlers bought from peddlers products that couldn't be made at home. For many years one of the best-selling items that peddlers offered was tinware. The amount of tinware displayed in the home reflected the family's wealth. This only encouraged manufacturers to think of other products they could make that would be appealing to the buyer. As the country became more progressive, giving its citizens opportunity for more leisure time, manufacturers noticed this and soon created objects, especially for children. They made toys for the beach, such as sand pails and shovels, and the Sandy Andy, a loading and dumping sand toy like those advertised in the 1921 Montgomery Ward catalog, priced to sell at $1.45.

Before the use of tin, manufacturers had been making toys out of wood and other natural materials. By 1840, however, tin became the favorite of manufacturers, because it was sturdy and lightweight. Tin plate that came from England was of a certain size, so the sand pails were the same, usually four and a half inches in diameter. Larger, thinner sheets of tin became available as the United States developed its own technology. By 1870, American factories produced more than forty thousand sand pails in one year.

A description in a 1920s Montgomery Ward catalog of a Sandy Andy toy.

At first the sand pails were painted by hand; then a technique called japanning became popular. This method used simply a couple of coats of paint followed by one coat of lacquer. Later, designs of children at play as well as holiday and patriotic themes were added to the sides of pails by using rubber stamps, stencils, and hand printing.

Wartime in particular affected both the production and the theme of sand toys. The Spanish-American War in 1898 catapulted Theodore Roosevelt into prominence. After the teddy bear was named for him during his presidency, reproductions of the bear appeared on sand pails. World War I interrupted the flow of German toys to the United States when factories in Germany were destroyed. By the end of that war in 1918, the United States dominated the toy industry. Added to the designs on sand pails in the twenties were airplanes, bicycles, motor cars, and steamships, all reflecting the progress of transportation during World War I.

During World War II in the forties, the government ordered production of all nonmilitary articles made of metal and rubber to cease for the war effort. These raw materials were necessary to build ships, planes, guns, and ammunition to fight against Germany, Italy, and Japan. When toy production resumed after the war, designs continued to show what had been popular in the thirties: Disney characters, barnyards, and circuses. Added to these were television personalities and space age scenes of the fifties. Plastics were developed in the sixties, and as a result, everything became . . . plastic. Other sand toys such as sand shovels, animal-shaped molds, and sifters were produced in bright colors. Today, tin toys are still popular but with collectors of antiques, a reflection of bygone years when everyone had a tin sand pail and shovel.

HORSE AND DUNE BUGGY RIDES

Horses as work animals played a major role in the actual development of the beach, pulling carts filled with sand to modify the shores. A hundred teams, each using eight horses, helped remove more than one hundred thousand cubic yards of sand and soil to excavate the Grand Canal in Venice, California.

In addition to being used as work animals, horses were ridden recreationally by couples who were romantically inclined. During the nineteenth century, horse and buggy rides on the

Horseback riding on the sand dunes at Pismo Beach, California; 1999.

beach were thought to be a prelude to a proposal. Later, there was nothing more thrilling than a horseback ride among the dunes. Dune buggies replaced horses and buggies for wild rides and races over sandy beach hills. When horse racing became a part of the beach scene, racehorses were cooled down with long walks in the refreshing waters of the ocean.

TENT CITY BY THE BEACH

Pismo Beach, California, is located on the central coast midway between Los Angeles and San Francisco. Quite literally a beach town, it has always filled the recreational needs of the county residents and tourists alike. In its early years, a city of tents and wagons blossomed on the beach each summer. Families arrived as early as May to set up housekeeping for days, weeks, or even months. Fish, clams, and mussels were available from the pier with just a little effort, and local farmers made regular rounds of the tents to peddle eggs, milk, and vegetables. Businesses specialized in leisure items such as bathing suits and fishing tackle.

At Pismo Beach children and adults learned to swim, but they observed special rules for sea bathing. One rule stated that "for a weak person, time enough to allow a few waves to pass over him will suffice."

In later years tent campers fondly recalled leisure time spent around campfires on one of the largest stretches of beach in California. The living was easy there, and the morning and evening fog brought relief from city heat. People came by horse and buggy from as far away as Fresno and Bakersfield in the Central Valley to spend their holidays in tent cities. Today, tourists from that same area come in vans and campers towing boats behind them. "Here comes the Bakersfield Navy," locals will say as a parade of boats floats across the desert intersected by Highways 46 and 41. But everyone understands. The beach is the place to be in the summertime, especially when you live in Bakersfield.

A Ferris wheel, horseback rides, and carriage rides offered choices of entertainment on Pismo Beach, California; late 1880s.

TAKING THE PLUNGE

As the nineteenth century became the twentieth, builders in American coastal cities began to construct large wooden buildings, about forty to seventy feet across, filled with cool green tidewater. In New York City these floating bathhouses or

The plunge at Santa Monica, California, gave beachgoers an opportunity for a different swim experience; early 1900s.

"plunges" were moored along the docks from Harlem to the Battery.

Millions of people used them during the hot, humid summers. Sweaty, exhausted bathers lined up at dawn, hoping for a refreshing swim that would last twenty minutes by the clock. Then a gong sounded and the next batch was allowed in. To linger or rebel brought cancellation of any further swimming privileges. Since most of the people who came to the bathhouses were immigrants and had little access to bathing or water entertainment, they quickly obeyed and thereby guaranteed their next opportunity to enjoy this activity.

These floating baths employed swimming instructors who were paid by the local board of education. Slowly, swimming became a national exercise among young men and women who were of a "progressive" mind.

In California, a few miles from Los Angeles, a group of

builders erected one bathing pavilion early in the twentieth century that looked like an ornate Arabian palace. Completed in eighteen months, it contained a saltwater plunge and hundreds of dressing rooms. Bathing suits were available to rent if bathers had come without their own. Just down the beach, plans were revealed in June 1905 for the Venice Bathhouse. It would be a three-story building of Spanish architecture with a saltwater plunge on the ground floor. Private baths and 520 changing rooms would occupy the top two floors to accommodate all the summer visitors expected on the new trolley lines from Los Angeles.

Gradually, other cities built municipal pools, or plunges, as the swimming craze spread throughout the nation. Jantzen Beach Park opened in May 1928 on the northern outskirts of Portland, Oregon. The swimming pools were a major attraction for the success of the park. For years the Jantzen Company had promoted swimming for health and beauty; therefore they made the pools a prominent feature at the park. More pools meant more people could swim if they weren't close to the beach. One pool was Olympic sized, another one was smaller for families, and there were also two children's pools for youngsters. Swim clubs can be considered a natural spinoff of these earlier municipal pools.

The area around the pool enclosure was covered with sand the first year and was called the Beach Park. The sand interfered with the filtration system, though, and was replaced with grass that fall. The pools continued to be popular until 1970 when the property was converted to a shopping center.

Swimming at a plunge in Jantzen Beach in Oregon allowed everyone in town a chance to cool off during the summer; 1928.

As swimming caught on, bathing houses multiplied to accommodate visitors. It seemed that more and more vacationers wanted to swim or at least splash around in the water to stay cool. The numbers of people who marched to the sea or pool in search of a good time grew quickly during the 1950s and 1960s. Going to the beach was rapidly becoming the number one sport in the nation.

CHAPTER SEVEN

From Sea to Shining Sea: So Many Beaches, So Little Time

CONEY ISLAND CHAOS

One thing can be said about Coney Island. There's never been a dull moment associated with it since Dutch explorers arrived in the fall of 1609, searching for a new route to the Spice Islands near India, China, and Japan. After colonizing the island, they completely dispossessed the established natives. The final insult to the Indians came when the Dutch named the island Konijn Hut, or rabbit's hutch, because of the great population of rabbits that inhabited the area. "Konijn" sounded somewhat like "coney," and the name quickly came into common use.

Coney Island as real estate changed hands and ownership many times over the next two hundred years until a group of Dutch descendants formed a company to build a road and a bridge. Included was a hotel for use in the summer. And so Coney Island's career as a resort began in 1829.

Coney Island took off slowly; the West End in particular was a lonely, quiet place. Surprisingly, that was just what many

Surf Avenue in Coney Island, New York, opened in 1880 and provided easier access to beach attractions; 1930s.

GREETING'S FROM CONEY ISLAND

visitors wanted. Not until after the Civil War did vacationers show an interest in the huge pavilions being built side by side down the island—which wasn't an island anymore, since the tidal creek that had separated it from the rest of Brooklyn had been filled in. No one minded. It made the resort easier to visit.

Although it was meant to be a place where families could spend their leisure time enjoying the surf and the sun, Coney Island began to look like the proverbial camel put together by a committee. In the early 1870s no one seemed to be in charge, so organizers and showmen took advantage of every opportunity to make easy money. Gamblers soon moved onto one end of the island, with liquor salesmen following closely behind. By the late 1800s, law-abiding citizens no longer felt safe and went home before dark. Politicians, too, had their moment making money on land deals. Soon Coney Island was a place to avoid rather than to visit.

But not for long. In 1894, lawbreaker John McKane was sent

to jail, and a reform movement began. Citizens insisted on a decent place to play, and Coney Island could be lucrative for this market if only the place was cleaned up. Soon hotels and restaurants were built near the original Coney Island House, all hoping to accommodate the masses. Because of the uniqueness of Lucy, Atlantic City's elephant-shaped attraction, Coney Island's entrepreneuers built a hotel also in the shape of an elephant. It was an enormous sculpture made of tin and wood, with spiral staircases in its hind legs, a cigar store in its front legs, and guest rooms in its body. The elephant hotel soon became a part of every visitor's itinerary before going on to gamble, drink, and attend shows that would have been X-rated by today's standard.

According to the newspaper ads, rides and novelty entertainments at Steeplechase Park, Coney Island, New York, kept everyone laughing and happy; circa 1907.

Finally someone came forward with ideas for entertainment for the entire family. A man named George C. Tilyou had grown up on the shores of Coney Island. As a youngster, he sold bottles of sand for a penny to visitors who wanted a real souvenir to take home. In 1897, he proceeded on his own vision of what Coney Island should be, and brought in equipment for a playground he named Steeplechase Park. He placed a Ferris wheel, an aerial slide, and a bicycle railway side by side. Not finished, he added double-dip chutes and the Barrel of Love, and pretended to blast pas-

Luna Park, Coney Island, New York, opened in May 1903 and was illuminated by more than one million lightbulbs. Called an "Electric Eden," it was destroyed by fire in the 1940s.

sengers into space by simulating a trip to the moon. Steeplechase became an instant hit and made a millionaire of Mr. Tilyou. When it was destroyed by fire in 1907, he put up a sign that read, "Admission to the burning ruins—10 cents." Then he rebuilt it, making it larger than before.

Two of his former employees became competitors when they opened Luna Park in 1903. When its 250,000 electric lights were turned on for the first time, the gathered crowd of 45,000 gasped loud enough to be heard on top of the Statue of Liberty. The community had gas lamps at home, so they'd never seen anything like this before. It was a dream of a payback for its owners. They recovered their $700,000 investment just six weeks after they opened the largest, most imaginative amusement park at Coney Island.

When the subway came to Coney in 1920, it brought the multitudes and more. People could now come by ferryboats, railroads, automobiles, and bicycles, and they did, as many as 200,000 on a single summer's day. Open from mid-May until early September, Coney Island attracted the rich and the poor, the immigrant and the native born, families and singles, old and young. It had something for everyone.

After the boardwalk was completed later in the twenties, the crowds had two miles of extra strolling space atop it and a smooching place below it. A nickel, or five pennies, got you everything Coney Island had to sell: a nickel to eat, a nickel to ride. Even during the Depression, 25 million people per season came for a nickel's worth of good time. Controlled fireworks exploded every Tuesday night off the shore from Coney Island. Girls and boys stood on rooftops of nearby apartment

The Coney Island waterfront along New York shores consisted of a five-mile stretch of sand and sea; date unknown.

houses to watch the Roman candle skies. During World Wars I and II, people needed the diversion more than ever. It seemed that nothing would ever change at Coney Island.

Then in 1944, everything did. Fire hit Luna Park and destroyed a great portion of it. The owners rebuilt sections, but it wasn't the same and it eventually closed for good in 1949. Coney Island continued, but change was in the air. Rides were torn down in favor of high-rise housing. Finally, Steeplechase Park closed.

Then came the revival. Old fans wouldn't let go of it, and gradually Coney Island began a comeback in the 1950s and 1960s. Today, visitors can go crabbing off the fishing pier, go to Coney and eat a candy apple while strolling the boardwalk, or ride one of the roller coasters. Throughout the year family attractions such as the Mermaid Parade in June, the hot-dog eating contest on July Fourth, and the Irish Fair on the week-end after Labor Day draw families to a last-of-the-season beach excursion.

GREAT SALTAIR BY GREAT SALT LAKE

In 1846, Brigham Young and his Mormon followers headed west from Nauvoo, Illinois, where they would be free of religious persecution. They settled in the Salt Lake Valley and soon founded Salt Lake City. On the Fourth of July, 1851, nearly the entire population of the small town traveled to the shores of Great Salt Lake to celebrate the holiday. The sixteen-mile trip took them about four hours by horse and buggy, which may have been the main reason a few of the more enter-prising citizens decided to build a railroad to the shore.

A visitor, writing home, said, "The Mormon people . . . intend building a Bathhouse and Hotel . . . which will make Great Salt Lake one of the greatest places of resort."

Why, then, did it take them more than twenty years to get the job done? No one knows, although journalists came by and placed their wordy blessings on the project. One British writer compared dipping in the salty lake to that of a "self-conscious gherkin [pickle] bathing in an aristocratic bath of condiments [pickle juice]."

That could have been the reason for the delay. Who wanted to feel like a pickle? Why didn't that writer tell it the way it was, that it was exhilarating to bob in the lake, its saline density keep-

With Saltair Pavilion in the background, bathers in the Great Salt Lake, Utah, show their buoyancy in the salty water; mid-1920s.

ing everyone afloat? "Look at me," faces seem to say in old photographs. "Look what I can do, and no swimming required!"

The lake is a remnant of prehistoric Lake Bonneville, which existed during the Ice Age. Four times as salty as the ocean, Salt Lake has varied greatly in size over the years, depending on the amount of rain and rate of evaporation. In 1873 it was 2,230 square miles; in 1901 it nearly disappeared.

As the city grew, it built a streetcar system with tracks running so close to the lake that John W. Young, one of Brigham Young's twenty-five sons, built some "pleasure grounds" on the shore. When the Utah and Nevada Railway was completed in 1875, the resort business really took off, and by the mid-1880s Garfield Beach and Black Rock were two of the most popular. But rivalries for patrons developed among the beach resort owners, leading William Glasmann to import a herd of buffalo to mingle with the folks at Buffalo Park. He found this was not a good marketing ploy. Few beachgoers were attracted to buffalo as sunning and swimming companions.

In 1893, building began on four thousand feet of railroad track laid on pilings straight out over the lake, which led to a Moorish-style two-story pavilion. When completed in June of that year, the resort was called Saltair. A restaurant and ballroom, said to be the largest in the world, occupied the top floor. There was no beach, so bathers stepped directly into the water. Thousands came to bathe, eat, and dance, making Saltair so desirable that other resorts suffered from lack of attendance.

No resort suffered as much as Garfield Beach when the building burned to the ground a decade later. Saltair had the resort business to itself after that until 1925, when it too burned down. However, a new resort quickly replaced the charred remains of the old.

That wasn't the worst problem. The Great Salt Lake had been receding for some time, and by the thirties, Saltair had a genuine beach, although not by its own choosing. Over the years its popularity rose and fell just like the level of the lake, but with the addition of amusement park-style attractions, Saltair remains one of the most visited resorts on the lake today. And no one feels like a pickle.

VENICE BEACH, CALIFORNIA

Abbot Kinney built a resort along a southern California beach near Los Angeles and opened it over the weekend of July

Ben Silver and a friend show off their athletic prowess on Venice Beach, California; around 1913.

Fourth, 1905. Although the concept of an amusement park by the sea is as American as baseball or root beer, Kinney chose to name his resort Venice after the beautiful Italian city built along a series of canals.

There were canals involved with the American Venice, too. Kinney and several partners had earlier built the Ocean Park resort nearby. Part of it contained wetlands, sand dunes, and marshes that sometimes flooded in winter. Dredging canals was one way of dealing with the marshy land. Kinney dreamed impossible dreams in addition to being a successful businessman. He saw the connection between the old and the new Venice and realized the association could be a romantic public relations tool.

Kinney came to California from the east, where Coney Island and Atlantic City were already established beach resorts. He quickly determined to build his own in his adopted state. Ocean Park became his first attempt, but he sold out to

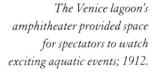

The Venice lagoon's amphitheater provided space for spectators to watch exciting aquatic events; 1912.

The Lagoon at Venice, Calif.

his partners and began Venice Beach by himself. In two years, dreams and business combined to make it one of the biggest attractions on the West Coast. A midway, bathing pavilions, roller coaster rides, a dance hall that had room for eight hundred couples, international pavilions with ongoing exhibits, gondola rides on the canals, and an aquarium were but a few of the many attractions that lured millions of visitors to Venice.

But all was not rosy in the land of Venice Beach. Control problems over money erupted between Kinney and his many associates, fires ignited, and World War I began. Then a flu epidemic hit right after the war. Attendance at the beach grew as if it were a place of refuge from the world's calamities. Finally, the city of Los Angeles took over and annexed Venice on November 25, 1925. Now the city's rules applied to all of the beach resort, forcing many of its offbeat or questionable exhibits to close.

The next years of the Great Depression and World War II impacted the entertainment at Venice Beach and finally Venice Pier closed in 1946. Code enforcement by the city caused the destruction of most of Venice's historic buildings. Although a nautical theme park opened in Ocean Park, it too closed in 1967.

But Venice would not die. In the seventies an unstructured midway became a tourist destination for those who had heard of the old Venice Beach and wanted to help in the rebirth of a place where the different and the daring could be free to express themselves. Bicyclists came first to use the new path built by the city. Weightlifters worked out at the Muscle Beach weight pen. Then a few entertainers arrived and began to play instruments, while others danced and sang.

Roller skating really put the revitalized Venice Beach on the map. Thousands soon were rolling down Ocean Front Walk, and visitors came to watch and be watched. The more unusual a person looked, the more he or she was noticed. Got a snake around your neck or a parrot on your shoulder? Rings in your nose or an electric guitar and amplifier on your back? Soon you'd have an audience.

The foodies moved in, and travel agents sold tours to beguile even more watchers. By 1984 Venice had become the number two tourist attraction in the state. (Disneyland was number one.) Since then it's been upgraded, downgraded, and revitalized once again. Acts like the chainsaw juggler and the man who plays two trumpets at the same time still find audiences. Venice is in business at the same old beach under the same old sun. Some things never die.

Strollers enjoy the Florida Space Coast; 1998.

OUT TO LAUNCH

It was just your average sand and ocean until May 5, 1961, when Alan Shepard in the Mercury spaceship *Freedom 7* blasted off into azure skies above a stretch of Florida's Atlantic coast. Sea turtle nesting sites and wildlife refuges had the place to themselves before high-flying six-million-pound spaceships carved out liftoff sites for their line of work. Now dune walkers wait for moon walkers along the sandy coast, arriving in RVs or vans to watch and wonder at this special kind of space at the beach.

Families who want to enjoy a space-launch holiday from one of these viewing beaches should plan ahead. Thousands of cars head for special viewing sites along AIA Highway, making it one grand parking lot for a few hours. Cocoa Beach Pier is a great place to view night launches, as well as the John F. Kennedy Space Center, although passes are needed to get in when there's a scheduled liftoff. More than 2,500 campground and RV sites from Titusville to Palm Bay provide seaside solitude and incredible views.

Either before or after the grand event there are plenty of things to do in and around this special section of beach. Cocoa

Beach and palm trees in Palm Beach, Florida, are typical attractions for visitors arriving on a relaxing holiday; date unknown.

Beach pier stretches 840 feet over the Atlantic Ocean and serves as a beachside grandstand for shuttle launches plus surfing and seafood festivals. Surfers worldwide know awesome waves at Cocoa, and three restaurants line the walkway along the pier. So do eager fishermen hoping for a big catch.

Surrounding the Kennedy Space Center is the 220-square-mile Merritt Island National Wildlife Refuge, which serves as home for endangered species such as the Western Indian manatee, the Southern bald eagle, and the Atlantic loggerhead turtle. Sand pines, saw palmettos, and live oaks that emerge from ancient sand dunes surround Turkey Creek Sanctuary in Palm Bay. A long boardwalk twists and turns along the murky, bass-filled black-water creek. The sanctuary is a major stopover for spring and fall migratory birds, including the pileated woodpecker and rare purple martin.

First, last, and best, however, is the beach. This seventy-two-mile Space Coast stretch along Florida's beaches has plenty of room to stretch for everyone.

CHAPTER EIGHT

Actors and Artists at the Beach: You Ought to Be in Pictures

Going to the beach has fascinated the American public for generations. As the fascination grew, and the impulse to record feelings about it grew as well, the beach filtered into all of the arts—music, painting, literature, theater, and film. As beach-goers changed their reasons for going to the beach from health to recreational, so have those attitudes been reflected in the arts.

A WALK ALONG THE WAVES

The nineteenth-century American writer Henry David Thoreau wrote of beach walks in a book titled *Cape Cod,* which is possibly one of the best books in American literature about the beach and its ever-changing faces.

Thoreau visited the beaches of Cape Cod four times, the first visit in October 1849 and the last in June 1857. More used to fresh water than salt, he had noticed the unbroken miles of sand on a map and decided this would be an interesting place to explore and complete his experience and education about the sea. Once there he didn't limit himself to the beach but also noted everything on the peninsula, including plants and birds.

On the first visit, which began October 11 in the rain, he said, "Everything told of the sea" even if it could not be seen or heard from the road above the beach. The rib of a whale had been woven into a roadside fence. Gulls wheeled overhead. Tall brush had been dwarfed by sea wind; orchards struggled in the salty atmosphere and soil.

But it was along the beaches that he wanted to be. He decided to walk twenty-five miles of uninterrupted shoreline along the Atlantic coast of Cape Cod from Eastham at one end of the peninsula to Provincetown at the other, taking three days to cover the distance. Although he carried a knapsack with a small

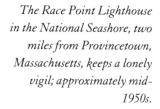

The Race Point Lighthouse in the National Seashore, two miles from Provincetown, Massachusetts, keeps a lonely vigil; approximately mid-1950s.

amount of food, Thoreau foraged along the way as well, finding small crustaceans to eat with his cache of bread.

Thoreau spent the first night of his trek with a Wellfleet oysterman and his family, recording the experience in easy-to-read prose that gives it a storylike quality. The second night of the three-day walk was spent with a lighthouse keeper, but not before exploring the land and the shore nearby. As he prepared to go inside for the evening he described a sunset that made him forget everything else he had just seen, noting "the shining torch of the sun [that] fell into the ocean." This is a quote from the Greek writer Homer as interpreted by Thoreau.

Today, Thoreau's walk is a well-marked hiker's paradise, now a part of the Cape Cod National Seashore. Happily the Cape remains similar to what Thoreau experienced over 140 years ago. Some of it is still pristine, isolated territory having escaped the scourge of urban development. The seascape reveals dunes and salt marshes, and great surfs crashing upon the beach, giving all the senses a feast of immeasurable beauty and sound. Thoreau called it "a sort of Promised Land."

Nearing the end of his walk Thoreau arrived at what is now Race Point Beach, two miles from Provincetown. Today, it's a great place to watch whales spouting offshore. Nearby is Beech Forest Trail, which circles a freshwater pond. Warblers from South America pack the area for two weeks in May, and it's also a beautiful trail to walk in autumn. Thoreau leaves us a picture through his words of this area as it once was, before modern intrusions.

STILL LIFE AND RESTLESS SEA

Everyone who's ever been to the beach knows that it is forever changing. The sand drifts, the waves crest and cascade, the wind carves trees and sand grass into new silhouettes. Once these scenes were trusted to memory only.

Then artists discovered the shore as subject, and the changing beach scenes soon took on permanence in their still lifes on canvas. Beach scenes actually began to appear in the 1820s from the brushes of a group of American landscape painters known as the Hudson River School. Located on the eastern seaboard, as their name implies, they experimented with reflected light on water. This technique illuminated, literally and figuratively, the scenes found between earth and water, sand and sky. Painters who used this technique were later called Luminists.

The American artist Alfred Thompson Bricher painted this beach scene, called "Baby Is King," in 1880. An oil on canvas, it can be seen at the Fine Arts Museum, San Francisco.

American painters traveled to Paris to further their studies using this technique. There they encountered artists of the Impressionist school who showed reflected light in their brush strokes as well, although their approach was more subdued. The American artists brought back this technique to interpret and use at home.

During the earlier part of the twentieth century, a true American style of painting emerged. It was brash and bright and called Realism, emphasizing social changes that were occurring not only at the beach but also in everyday life. Descendants of the Dutch settlers on the eastern seaboard came from a land that floated on water. The earliest maritime scenes showing life on the sea depicted a realism that seemed nearly tangible.

As scenes on the beach progressed through the twentieth century from sedate to fashionable to gaudy and scandalous,

This etching of a Coney Island beach by Reginald Marsh is an example of the Realist movement that swept the nation early in the twentieth century; 1935.

pop culture artists such as Reginald Marsh recorded them. Finally, camera operators became artists in film, thereby establishing a new artistic medium. Today, some photographs of scenes that found their way into Marsh's works are considered art in themselves.

SINGING SONGS OF THE SEA

While the beach grew in favor as a vacation destination, it also leaped in popularity as a subject for leading songs of the day. The late nineteenth and early twentieth centuries rang with music, but it was heard by few. Radios were still so new and full of static that not many people owned them; movies had no voice and therefore no music; Thomas Edison was just getting around to inventing recordings. Meanwhile, music stores in every town across the country hired piano players to pound out the latest tunes for local customers. The music that most people heard came from their own parlors or the concert and marching bands on tour in the summertime.

The sheet music that folks bought in music stores to play at home reflected the excitement and romance at the beach that they hoped to experience. "Skate with Me, Kate (at the Million Dollar Pier)" was a hit in 1903. In 1905, a song inspired by rolling chairs became hummable along the beach at Atlantic City. Called "Why Don't You Try" or "The Rolling Chair Song," the tune supposedly produced romantic tingling in the hearts of all who heard it. "By the Light of the Silvery Moon" sounded best if the moon was shining on water, particularly a lake or an ocean. "On the Pier," composed in 1926, gave many citizens who would never have a chance to visit the sea an opportunity to visit vicariously through music. "On the Boardwalk in Atlantic City" could be heard all over the country, as could "Coney Island Baby." Bert Parks introduced the song "There She Is, Miss America" in 1955, making the song forever synonymous with the Miss America pageant. A nearly forgotten 1957 movie called *Bernardine* starring Pat Boone and Terry Moore had little to offer but the romantic song "Love Letters on the Sand." Boone recorded it as a single title and it became a hit.

The Beach Boys were a major socioeconomic phenomenon of the sixties, creating a musical myth about the surf and sand life that some participants still inhabit. As soon as they recorded "Surfer Girl" in 1963, the Beach Boys became a household name, especially if the household was near a California beach. It didn't take them long to become nationally and then internationally recognized. With songs like "Summer Days" recorded in 1965 and "Surf's Up" in 1971, they leaped into the record books to stay.

Citizens who could actually go to major beach resorts were treated to a variety of musical performances. First there was vaudeville in the late 1800s featuring animal acts, musical revues, and comedy sketches. As piers were built, their owners vied to produce musical concerts featuring such talent as John Philip Sousa and his marching band, or beginners like Paul Whiteman and his orchestra; Whiteman would later introduce

"By the Light of the Silvery Moon" was a popular song of the early 1920s.

Ray Charles entertains at the Club Harlem on North Kentucky Avenue in Atlantic City, New Jersey; around 1960.

the compositions of George Gershwin. In the thirties, a young bandleader named Harry James and his orchestra played some dates on Steel Pier in Atlantic City. He brought a band singer with him named Frank Sinatra. The beat went on.

Many African-American performers began at Coney Island or Atlantic City. The Paradise Club off the boardwalk introduced Nat King Cole, Billy Eckstine, Count Basie, and Ray Charles. A performer named Peg Leg Bates danced and somersaulted while wearing different-colored artificial legs that matched his tuxedos. Vicki Gold Levi's book *Atlantic City* quotes a drummer named Chris Columbo as saying that at the Paradise Club "the entertainment was 90 percent black and the trade [audience] was 90 percent white."

LIGHTS! CAMERA! ACTION!

More than a hundred beach movies were filmed during the 1960s. *Beach Party,* produced by American International in 1963 and starring Annette Funicello, was typical. The films had formula plots: boy meets girl at the beach; they sing, they dance, they kiss then fight, then kiss and make up while dancing and singing some more about the whole experience. All the while, platoons of singers and dancers are jumping to a rock and roll beat in the background. Production costs were low because the beach was the setting and swimsuits the costumes. You've seen one, you've seen them all, but it didn't matter.

Actress Annette Funicello is shown on location with other actors for the movie Beach Party, *produced in 1963.*

During their day, the beach movies and their stars were better known than any other phenomenon in the teenagers' universe. Annette Funicello, Sandra Dee, and Frankie Avalon seemed to appear in most of these movies, with the ever present Beach Boys, of course. Elvis Presley starred in the rest. Nothing more was needed except popcorn and a date.

Beaches, particularly those associated with historical events, have appeared as background for many other motion pictures. Orson Welles photographed scenes for his masterpiece *Citizen Kane* at Atlantic City, and the 1953 movie *From Here to Eternity* contained a love scene on the beach that is forever remembered by movie fans of that period. Finally, the recent film *Saving Private Ryan* opens with an invasion scene on the Normandy coast during World War II that is unforgettable in its re-creation.

Beaches in songs, words, or pictures remain forever etched in our collective memory. It's no surprise that the drama of the beach speaks to us all through artistic expression.

CHAPTER NINE

Hot Jobs and Cold Facts: Summer Work and Safety

CONSTABLES OF THE SURF

Many teenagers would like to get summer jobs as lifeguards. What a life! Summer at the beach, sitting around in the shade, hanging out with friends, and getting paid for it as well. But there's much more to it than that.

Lifesaving probably had its origins along the sandbars off

A lady "Constable of the Surf" admonishes beachgoers about their daring costumes; 1920s.

Cape Cod. More than a thousand ships piled up there in the late 1700s, and frequently passengers drowned, sometimes just a couple hundred yards from the beach. Volunteers from local towns had few skills to save them back then. In 1797, the Massachusetts Humane Society erected huts along the most dangerous sections of the coast, hoping that stranded sailors who made it ashore on their own would find them and take shelter. Not until 1872 did the government put a lifesaving service into operation. Stations were built five miles or so apart on the beach, and surfmen kept a constant lookout.

When the surfmen sighted a ship's distress signal, the rescuers fired a red light in response to let the crew at sea know that rescue was on the way. Then the lifesaving crew jumped into action. They launched special surfboats, some equipped with air chambers, cork fenders, and righting lines. If the ship-

A 1907 photograph shows rescuers removing a captain and his mate from a breeches buoy, the last two to leave a sinking ship.

wreck happened close enough to shore, the team stayed on the beach and used a contraption called a breeches buoy.

The breeches buoy was essentially a large life ring. Canvas covered the center, with two holes in it for the seaman's legs, sort of like a pair of pants. The rider hung his legs through the holes, with the ring supporting him under his armpits. How he got to shore was a more complex matter. Using a small cannon called a Lyle gun, the surfmen fired a double line with a pulley to the ship, connecting it to the surfmen on shore. Back and forth the breeches buoy went on the line, carrying seamen to safety. Even during the summer months today, National Seashore Rangers at Race Point in Provincetown give a weekly demonstration of a breeches buoy drill to show visitors how it was done.

GUARDING LIVES

Lifeguards for swimmers first appeared at Atlantic City in 1855. The first "Constable of the Surf" was paid $117 for the entire summer. Captain William Tell Street came on the scene in 1870 with his patented "life lines for surf bathing." He'd invented the device—heavy cables fastened to pilings on the beach and running to anchors offshore. Not until two years later did volunteer lifeguards patrol the beach, and it wasn't until twenty years later that the city finally ponied up for a paid lifeguard patrol. They sat in boats offshore, watching that no one swam out beyond the floats marking the edge of the designated swim area; most of those rescued had done just that. The swimmers overlooked the fact that they had to turn around

and swim back as well. As one lifeguard put it, they forgot that the ocean has only one side and not four like a swimming pool.

In the late 1800s, as the idea of a day at the beach caught on, more people went to the beach and, unfortunately, many drowned because they lacked water skills and safety knowledge. Super surfer George Freeth moved to the mainland from Hawaii in 1907 to become a lifeguard at Redondo Beach, California. Standing on a Venice pier one stormy day in December 1908, he noticed a fleet of Japanese fishing boats bobbing in Santa Monica Bay. Realizing instantly that they were in trouble, he threw himself into the waves, swam out to the boats, and helped rescue eleven fishermen. He earned a Congressional Medal for his efforts and even more admirers than he'd had before. When Duke Paoa Kahanamoku from Hawaii visited California in 1913, he introduced his redwood surfboard to Long Beach lifeguards. Later, surfboards came to be used as rescue devices by lifeguards everywhere.

Since the government still did not promote lifesaving training programs at this time, private organizations such as the Young Men's Christian Association and the American Red Cross did. The Red Cross adopted the motto "Everyone a swimmer, every swimmer a lifesaver." Police and fire departments of many cities soon included lifesaving in their emergency training techniques. Finally, by the end of the 1930s more public beaches employed lifeguards.

During World War II, six women were hired to serve as lifeguards at Atlantic City, but it was a short-lived experiment. Men yelled from the ocean that they were drowning just so the attractive women would attempt to rescue them. Today, there are many female lifeguards on major beaches hired not only to comply with fair employment practices, but mainly because their skills are as competent as men's.

After World War II, rescue flotation devices that had been developed as early as 1897 were refined and made safer. However, even these devices from the 1940s to the 1960s had problems. They were easily punctured and became waterlogged. Finally, in 1972 a lifeguard named Steve Morgan designed a flotation device that is still in use. Shaped like a torpedo and made of hard plastic, the device has handles that can easily be grasped by victims and rescuers alike.

Today's lifeguards go through rigorous training before they can become "constables." The city of Los Angeles started a lifeguard corps in 1916. Now it's run by the Los Angeles County Fire Department. Seven hundred lifeguards work during the summer months, and about 110 of those work the year round.

The United States Lifesaving Association was established in 1979 to maintain high standards for open water lifeguards and to promote the saving of human life in and around the aquatic environment. Minimum standards must be met, and lifeguards have to meet recommended qualifications. Briefly, according to the *United States Lifesaving Association Manual of Open Water Lifesaving,* these are: Open water lifeguards should be at least sixteen years old. They must have training in first aid and emergency medical care. They must also have training in cardiopulmonary resuscitation and must successfully complete all training course requirements of the hiring agency. Lifeguards must be able to swim at least 500 meters over a measured course in ten minutes or less. Health and fit-

Lifeguards keeping vigilant watch over a massive crowd on a Chicago lakefront beach; 1980s.

ness must be adequate for the stresses of lifesaving, and scuba training is necessary in some circumstances.

SAFETY FIRST, LAST, AND ALWAYS

It's easy to forget about safety at the beach because there are too many enjoyable things to think about and do, like showing off for the cute girl or guy on the next beach towel. On an excitement scale, reviewing safety rules ranks right up there with a visit to the dentist. Yet it's a necessary part of going to the beach, so let's plunge in and learn to be safe.

As discussed in chapter five, kite flying at the beach is an adventure, but like all adventures, it's best to be prepared for it. Experts on the subject have a few tips: Consider the ocean's distance when flying a kite. Sneaker waves can rise up hundreds of feet farther on the beach and sweep everything away, especially string and plastic bags. Birds and sea life can become entangled in discarded paraphernalia and lose their lives.

Most people believe kiters have to run to launch their kites, yet that's when most accidents occur. Watching their kites may land the kiters in a hole dug in the sand, or slammed up against a tree or another person. If the wind is steady and strong enough, even as mild as five to ten miles per hour, no running is required. If kiters can feel a breeze on their faces, they should have enough wind to loft a standard kite.

BRING A BUDDY

Disaster is always around the corner. Or so they say. The best swimmers on the school team still should swim only at beaches protected by lifeguards. They also need to swim with a buddy. The waves may look inviting, the sea may look calm and peaceful, but both the Pacific Ocean and the Atlantic Ocean can be misleading. Here's what John Clark, the experienced surfer we met in chapter five, has to say on the subject:

When I was a teenager, I started surfing big waves on the North Shore [of Oahu]. My friends and I surfed all the famous sites like the Banzai Pipeline and Sunset Beach. One day we were out at one of the North Shore sites called Laniakea. I caught a four-foot wave and made my turn as the wave lined up in front of me. I saw that this wave was going to tube, so I moved up on my board and crouched down as the lip of the wave pitched over me. After a couple of seconds I realized that the wave was outrunning me and that I wasn't going to make it out of the tube, so I bailed to get away from my board.

The wave, however, picked up my board and shot it right back at me. The board's fin struck me on the back of my head, opening a deep gash. I saw stars from the impact, but luckily I wasn't knocked unconscious. Head wounds always bleed a lot and this one was no exception. I left a trail of blood in the water all the way into the beach. We jumped in our car and drove to a nearby clinic where the doctor put in ten stitches to close the wound.

My friends still wanted to surf so we drove back to Laniakea. The waves were still good but no one was in

John Clark surfing on Wailupe Beach, Oahu, with Diamond Head in the background; 1996.

the water. When we asked what was happening, the guys told us that, right after we left, a huge tiger shark had come right through the surf following my trail of blood, so everyone cleared out of the water. In all my years of surfing, that was as close as I've ever come to a tragic accident. It taught me two things: that you have to know how to swim to be a surfer and that you should never surf alone. No matter how good you are, accidents happen.

Advice from the nearest lifeguard should be considered carefully before jumping into the ocean. If the lifeguard station is too far away for a tête-à-tête, look at the colored flags flying from the station. Flags send a distinct message by their colors: green, it's safe to swim; yellow indicates caution; red means no swimming allowed, and blue warns that stinging jellyfish are present.

Man-o'-wars love the ocean when it's warmest, so watch out

for them between April and November. And stay far away too; tentacles extend from the bubble and can cause a painful sting. If stinging occurs, see a lifeguard right away. He or she will know how to provide simple first aid to relieve the sting.

Riptides form a strong current surge through sandbar troughs on the ocean floor. A frothy river of water begins to run perpendicular to the shoreline. If swimmers get caught in a riptide, their first reaction is to fight the tide and head for shore. Usually they are going straight against the tide. Even the strongest swimmers can't outswim a riptide. Swimmers who are caught in a riptide should try to stay calm and swim parallel to shore. The rhythmic motion of the waves will guide the swimmers back into shore. If there's any question about riptides, lifeguards should be asked immediately. They may even have a special flag to fly for them.

Other safety precautions from lifeguards concern "sneaker

Going to the beach with a buddy; 1920s.

waves," and this doesn't mean Nikes or Reeboks. Sudden wave surges, called sneaker waves, can wash along the shore with enough force to knock a person down, even to drag someone out to sea. This is something to be aware of because it comes as such a surprise.

Substituting floating devices, such as a pair of Swimmies, for swimming ability is not a good idea. Stay in water that's knee to waist deep if you're not a strong swimmer. Watch out not only for wave sizes and tides but for bottom troughs, or "crab holes," as well. And it can't be stressed enough to always have a buddy.

Many beaches lie along isolated, rugged oceanfronts. Their natural beauty is appealing, but they can be even more deadly than the smooth carpets of sand that are most familiar to the beachgoer. Hiking into beach coves without knowing tidal

Laguna Beach is one of California's most beautiful beaches, but it can also be treacherous when rough rocks and waves collide; postcard circa 1940.

schedules or climbing out on dangerous headlands and onto shaky cliffs can result in tragedy. Adventurers not only place themselves in jeopardy, but also disrupt local wildlife and damage the environment. The Cannon Beach, Oregon, Chamber of Commerce reminds us that "nature is not a theme park." Wise words to remember, especially at the beach.

CHAPTER TEN

Are Beaches Here to Stay?
Uses and Misuses

Will we always have beaches, and will we always want to visit them? Or will they become garbage dumps, ecological messes that ooze with contamination? Even now, children find hypodermic needles washed up onshore from medical dumpsites. Other beaches have to be closed for weeks because leaks from refuse plants drift onto public shores. Is there anything we can do to slow or stop the desecration of our beaches?

Coastlines are among the richest and the most fragile areas on our planet. Beach safety and ecology should be on our minds when we go to the beach as visitors. How we respect the beach reflects how we will treat it. Many ecological programs show us how to care for nature's gift.

The Respect the Beach organization has evolved from the nationwide Surfrider Foundation. It's a coastal educational program designed to "teach the basics of marine ecology, coastal stewardship, and beach safety." Students from kindergarten through twelfth grade learn how they can improve the

experience of going to the beach for themselves and everyone, and for the plants and animals who live there. Beach cleanup and storm drain stenciling are two ways this program assists in coastal ecology.

A similar organization is the Malibu Foundation for Environmental Education, which created California Oceans Day. In honor of a recent Oceans Day in May 2000, more than 4,000 boys and girls descended on beaches in California to clean them, and they became involved in recycling and litter-reduction programs. The children also helped promote the "Whale Tail" license plate. So far, more than 38,000 drivers have purchased Whale Tail license plates, which help fund the program.

Everyone knows about beach cleanups. People volunteer regularly to patrol sections of the beach and pick up man-made debris. By reading local newspapers and listening to radio and television stations, volunteers can find out what's going on in the areas nearest them.

The Seaventure Resort in Pismo Beach, California, makes it easy to volunteer. It has a regular beach cleanup program that meets on the second Saturday of every month. High school students, senior citizens, and families gather at the hotel, enjoy a hot drink and snack, then collect bags and gloves and go to work. They gather styrofoam, cigarette butts, old socks, picnic remnants, and even dead fowl. It's a helpful way to spend a morning at the beach and make it cleaner for everyone.

Storm drain stenciling is another volunteer program, not as well-known as beach cleanups. "Dump No Waste—Protect Your Water" is stenciled next to storm drains as a clear warning that all water flowing into storm drains goes unfiltered directly to the sea. Thirty-three percent of beach closures have

Volunteers in the Adopt a Beach program collect refuse to make the beach cleaner and safer for everyone; 1998.

occurred in recent years because of street runoff after a heavy rain. Believe it or not, more oil has drained into the ocean from street runoffs due to car leaks than from oil tanker spills. By stenciling the warning message next to drains, volunteers hope the public will begin to understand that what they drop on the street today, they may swim in tomorrow. A pending bill in

Congress will establish a national ocean-water quality standard that can be monitored not only by the government but by citizens as well.

BE AWARE OF WETLANDS

Wetlands have been defined as nature's water filters. They protect our oceans and bays from polluted runoffs. As rainwater drains, it picks up pollutants on its way to the sea, pollutants from such household sources as fertilizers and pesticides, soapy water from washing machines, oil and antifreeze from cars, and feces from pets. Swamps and marshes, which are wetlands, slow the drainage. Heavier sediments settle at the bottom of those swamps and marshes while the filtered water sinks into the ground and replenishes our drinking supplies. The roots of the wetland plants soak up heavier materials and pollutants.

However, many natural wetlands have now been paved over. The parking lot at the beach you visit may once have been a wetland. If you live near a beach, your house or apartment may have been built on filled wetland. The U.S. Environmental Protection Agency tells us that 51 percent of the nation's wetlands have disappeared and estimates that the nation is losing one million acres of wetlands every ten years. Should we care? You bet.

Wetlands support biologically rich areas, teeming with life. Fish spawn and birds lay eggs in wetlands. Birds use them as resting

Gulls are visitors to the nation's wetlands.

places during their north and south migrations between winter and summer homes. Many species of birds and fish will become extinct without wetlands. It's frightening to think about, but it's possible that our beaches could become extinct as well.

So, what do we do?

A POLLUTION SOLUTION

Treat the beach as if it belonged to you because, in a way, it does. It needs our love and protection just as our own private living places do. We can become beachcombers to protect the coastal shores. However, instead of looking for beautiful artifacts to take home, we can look for harmful objects to remove, including what we have brought with us. It's important to pack out what we have carried in, including kite string, discarded fishing gear, food wrappers, and all plastic containers and bottles. Take photographs, leave only your footprints on the sand.

Everything that calls the beach or nearby wetlands home needs to be respected and protected. Some beaches are fortunate to have a diverse ecosystem with forested areas not far away. Wild animals from those wooded areas sometimes wander onto coastal beaches or into wetlands. Watch them from a distance; give them space and respect their territory. Don't try to feed them or frighten them, as they may abandon their young. Worse, if

These feet are made for walking on the beach; 1980.

frightened or concerned about their young families, animals may go on the attack.

Swimming and surfing reveal more life just under the waves. A wide variety of fish, depending on where you live, may swim with you for curiosity. In California waters, dolphins sometimes make their presence known as they cavort by your side, but be reluctant to join their games; they're bigger than you are. Occasionally, dolphins and whales beach themselves, and no one knows why. Great effort is made to return these animals to the sea in condition to care for themselves; sometimes they are found too late.

SHE SELLS SEA SHELLS BY THE SEASHORE

On the beach, gatherers of shells walk a fine line between collecting and scavenging. Should shells be collected at all? Should they be removed from the beach, their natural habitat? Many people agree with N. Scott Rugh, Manager of Invertebrate Fossils Collections at the San Diego Natural History Museum. He says, "It's okay for young people to collect empty

Famous Pismo Beach clams (left); 1998. A bat star with baby limpet (right); 1998.

shells so that they can learn about ocean life; to know it is to love it and then, protect it."

He goes on to say that "In general, there are no restrictions against collecting empty shells from California beaches. However, on some beaches, empty shells may *not* be collected. Two examples are the La Jolla Ecological Reserve in San Diego County and Point Lobos State Reserve in central California, where it's forbidden to remove live animals, empty shells, and even rocks."

But what about collecting mollusks (living shellfish)? With a fishing license in California, diving to collect living shells is permitted 1,000 feet from shore. However, there are bag limits and seasons for some mollusks such as abalone. A license is required for collecting living shells on the beach also.

On Assateague Beach, in Chincoteague, Virginia, the National Park Service limits the number of unoccupied shells collected to one gallon per visit and does not allow shells to be used for commercial purposes. Galveston, Texas, beach officials request also that no living shells be collected. The State of Florida has restrictions, too, as do all states where seashells are found in their natural habitat. It's best to check the fish and game regulations of each state and with local authorities before removing any form of sea life from the beach.

And keep in mind that saltwater life and freshwater life are vastly different, and animals taken from one cannot survive in the other. Many young enthusiasts collect at the beach for aquariums at home, then wonder why their specimens die. It's a hard lesson to be learned by everyone.

WHOSE BEACH IS IT ANYWAY?

Marine animals such as seals and sea lions spend time on beaches and offshore rocks because that is a part of their natural habitat. People need to think about who the visitor is and who the resident is, then act accordingly. If a sick, injured, or dead animal is found, contact the local authorities. Hopefully, a lifeguard or beach patrol officer will be nearby and can help.

Beaches are habitats for some creatures that can hardly be seen without magnifiers. Many of those organisms are vital to the ecosystem of their environment. Take care not to step on marine life or remove those sand creatures from their natural habitat. There can be a great variety of sea stars, anemones, crabs, limpets, and other living organisms in the tide pools and exposed areas at low tide. Remember that even barnacles are alive. Through research it's been proven that it takes only two hundred people walking over the same spot to kill whatever is living there. When that spot on the beach is damaged, seven or more years are needed for the place to recolonize and recover

Unusual activities, such as the prizefights held on a Galveston, Texas, beach, sometimes dramatically increase foot traffic; date unknown.

before life is restored. Federal law now protects many areas, so while observing nature, observe the laws that govern its safety.

Look around. How many people are on the beach right now? How many will there be tomorrow or the coming weekend? Take a look at one of the pictures of crowded beaches in this book and try to count the number of people who are congregated there. In the summertime, it's quite common to have two hundred thousand visitors a day at any of the nation's larger beaches. It's no wonder that not much is left alive after that many feet have walked on minuscule sea creatures that call the beach their home.

Young people can participate in coast watch programs and adopt a portion of a beach or wetland to protect. Some adopters track natural changes and human impact and can learn where to take information when problems arise. This can become a project for Boy Scouts, Girl Scouts, science classes at school, and even families. Church and synagogue young people's organizations will also find this an opportunity to participate. Saving our heritage for future generations and practicing stewardship of nature's habitats should be the goal of every person who steps onto the beach.

A beach alone and at rest, Lake Michigan, near Frankfort, Michigan; 1980.

CHAPTER ELEVEN

The Top Ten List Parade: Can Anyone Decide?

Now for the lists. Here are some of my favorite beaches for walking, swimming, snorkeling, windsurfing, shell collecting, and other activities. These lists are meant to be only the beginning, the jumping-off point for you to start creating your own lists.

TOP TEN BEACHES

Wailea Beach, Hawaii

Harris Beach State Park, Oregon

Newport Beach, California

Clearwater Beach, Florida

St. Joseph Peninsula State Park, Florida

Rehoboth Beach, Delaware

Kaunaoa, Hawaii

Ocracoke Island, North Carolina

East Hampton Beach, Long Island, New York

Carpinteria City Beach, California

TOP TEN URBAN BEACHES

South Beach, Miami Beach, Florida

Waikiki Beach, Oahu, Hawaii

Panama City Beach, Florida

East Beach, Santa Barbara, California

Newport Beach, California

Myrtle Beach, South Carolina

South Padre Island, Texas

Cape May, New Jersey

Main Beach, Santa Cruz, California

Seaside Beach, Oregon

TOP TEN BEACHES FOR WINDSURFING

Maui, Hawaii (Kehei/Kanaha/Ho'okipa)

Oahu, Hawaii (Kailua Bay/Diamond Head)

Corpus Christi, Texas/South Padre Island

Columbia River Gorge, Oregon

Cape Hatteras, North Carolina (Pamlico Sound)

San Francisco, California (Coyote Point/Crissy Field)

Puerto Rico (Ponce)

U.S. Virgin Islands (Sapphire Beach)

Santa Cruz, California

Baja California (Los Barriles/San Carlos)

TOP TEN BEACH MOVIES

South Pacific (1958)

On the Beach (1959)

How to Stuff a Wild Bikini (1965)

Jaws (1975)

Endless Summer (1980)

The Beach Girls (1982)

Where the Boys Are (1984)

Brighton Beach Memoirs (1986)

Muppet Treasure Island (1996)

The Beach (2000)

TOP TEN SONGS ABOUT THE BEACH

"Love Letters in the Sand" (Pat Boone, 1957)

"Surfin' USA" (The Beach Boys, 1963)

"Under the Boardwalk" (The Drifters, 1964)

"(Sittin' on) The Dock of the Bay" (Otis Redding, 1967)

"Summertime's Calling Me" (The Catalinas, 1975)

"I Love Beach Music" (The Embers, 1979)

"Myrtle Beach Days" (Fantastic Shakers, 1980)

"Vacation" (Go-Go's, 1982)

"One Particular Harbor" (Jimmy Buffet, 1983)

"Thong Song" (Sisqo, 2000)

TOP TEN BEACHES FOR SURFING

Cape Hatteras Lighthouse Beach, North Carolina

Waimea Bay Beach, Oahu, Hawaii

Seaside Beach, Oregon

Rincon Beach, Santa Barbara, California

Steamers, Santa Cruz, California

Ditch Plains Beach, East Hampton, Long Island, New York

Delmarva Indian River North Beach, Delaware

Sebastian Inlet, Florida

Maverick, Half Moon Bay, California

Santa Rosa Island, Florida

TOP TEN BEACHES FOR VOLLEYBALL

Manhattan Beach, California

South Padre Island, Galveston, Texas

Santa Monica Beach, California

East Beach, Santa Barbara, California

Santa Cruz, California

Myrtle Beach, South Carolina

North Avenue Beach, Chicago, Illinois

Clearwater, Florida

Virginia Beach, Virginia

Belmar, New Jersey

TOP TEN BEACHES FOR STROLLING

Sanibel Island, Florida

Carmel Beach, California

Long Beach, Washington

Green Sand Beach, Big Island, Hawaii

Hammocks Beach State Park, North Carolina

Brighton Beach, Brooklyn, New York

Venice Beach, Venice, California

Old Silver Beach, Cape Cod, Massachusetts

Jones Beach, Long Island, New York

Oak Street Beach, Chicago, Illinois

TOP TEN BEACHES FOR SAND COLLECTING

Hokuula, Maui

Puu Mahana, Hawaii

Waipio Valley, Hawaii

Singer Island, Florida

Waimea, Oahu

Point Reyes, California

Whales Head Cove, Oregon

Fort Bragg, California

Bar Harbor, Maine

Cape Hatteras, North Carolina

TOP TEN PIERS FOR FISHING

Dauphin Island, Dauphin Island, Alabama

Santa Monica Pier, Santa Monica, California

Okaloosa Island Pier, Fort Walton Beach, Florida

Cape Porpoise Pier, Kennebunkport, Maine

Shantytown Fishing Pier, Ocean City, Maryland

Keansburg Fishing Pier, Keansburg, New Jersey

Avalon Fishing Pier, Kill Devil Hills, North Carolina

Dirty Pelican Fishing Pier, Gilchrist, Texas

Lake Geneva Fishing Pier, Lake Geneva, Wisconsin

Tramp Harbor Fishing Pier, Seattle, Washington

TOP TEN BEACHES FOR BUILDING SAND CASTLES

Fiesta Island, San Diego, California

Ocean City Beach, Ocean City, Maryland

Treasure Island Beach, Treasure Island, Florida

Imperial Beach, Imperial Beach, California

Cannon Beach, Cannon Beach, Oregon

Myrtle Beach, South Carolina

Rehoboth Beach, Dewey, Delaware

Hulopoe Beach, Lanai, Hawaii

Sandspur Beach, Bahia Honda Key, Florida

Galveston Island, Texas

TOP TEN BEACHES FOR SCUBA DIVING

Monterey Bay, California

Kona Coast, Hawaii

Panama City, Florida

Eden Rock, Grand Cayman, Cayman Islands

CoCo View, Roatan, Honduras

La Ceiba, Cozumel, Mexico

Black Rock, Hawaii

Bonaire, Netherlands Antilles

La Jolla, California

Paradise Reef, Cozumel, Mexico

Chronology

ANCIENT MAN

EGYPTIAN EXODUS PERIOD

1175 B.C. Invasion of Egypt by Confederation of Sea Peoples, including the Greeks. They see the Egyptians relaxing in the Nile and take the idea home with them.

500 B.C. Emergence of Greek civilization. Citizens enjoy science, math, literature, the arts, and practicing hygiene

484–424 B.C. Herodotus chronicles Greek history

Second century to first century B.C. Civilization of Greece gradually declines, and Romans take over world leadership

49 B.C. Julius Caesar rises to power in Rome

47 B.C. Julius Caesar tries to conquer Egypt by defeating Ptolemy XIII at Alexandria

77 A.D. Romans conquer Britain

Fourth century A.D. Romans build luxurious villas using mosaics that depict female figures wearing bathing costumes

450–750 Dark Ages, approximately

476 Collapse of Roman Empire

1400s TO 1500 Explorers go to the New World

1538 Nicolas Wynman writes first paper about swimming

1587 Everard Digby writes a book of swimming instructions

1609 Dutch explorers land on Konijn Hut (Coney Island); resort begins in 1829

1620 Pilgrims land on Cape Cod, Massachusetts

1759 Richard Russell publishes a paper on uses of seawater

1776 Thirteen American colonies declare independence

1777 Explorers see surfers in Polynesia

1781 Revolutionary War ends in thirteen colonies

1797 Massachusetts Humane Society begins to help stranded sailors

Early 1800s Vincent Priessnitz begins Water University theories

1804 Lewis and Clark voyage begins

1805–1806 Lewis and Clark establish salt-making activity on Seaside Beach

1820s Hudson River School of artists organizes to paint beach scenes

1830s U.S. Industrial Revolution begins, after Eli Whitney's cotton gin (patented in 1794) becomes the first of many inventions to bring about mass production

Mid–nineteenth century British invent diving platforms

1849 Henry David Thoreau visits Cape Cod for the first time

1851 Mormons of Salt Lake City decide to build a bathhouse on the shores of the Great Salt Lake

1860s Purchase of Absecon Island (later Atlantic City)

1870 Sand pails produced by the thousands

1870 First boardwalk built in Atlantic City at a cost of five thousand dollars

1872 Lifesaving services begin operating in Massachusetts

1876 Americans display rolling chairs at Philadelphia Centennial

1881 Lucy the elephant built, Atlantic City, New Jersey

1882 Saltwater taffy named, Atlantic City, New Jersey

1893 Lifeguards serve at Rainbow Beach, Chicago, for the first time

1893–1933 National Weather Service operates kite stations

1895 Volleyball introduced

1897 Philip McCord becomes first recognized sand castle builder

1903 Luna Park at Coney Island opens

1905 Sears Roebuck shows two swimsuits in its catalog

1905 Resort opens in Venice, California

1907 Annette Kellerman designs first practical swimsuit

1910 Jantzen Company produces first swimsuit

1917 United States enters World War I; civilian manufacture converts to war production

1921 First Miss America contest held in Atlantic City

1923 Jantzen red diving girl becomes first successful swimsuit logo

1928 A swimsuit industry is born

1929 Stock market crash in United States

1941 United States enters World War II; all civilian manufacture converts to war production

1945 World War II ends; swimsuit industry begins again

1946 Bikini swimsuit first appears on beaches

1946 Venice Pier closes

1952 Sandcastling contests begin at Ft. Lauderdale, Florida, beach

1960s Beach music and movies become popular

1967 Ocean Park, California, closes

1968 Windsurfing becomes a sport

1970s Professional surfing introduced and canine Frisbee begins

1972 Flotation device to save lives introduced

1979 United States Lifesaving Association established

1984 Venice, California, experiences resurgence in popularity and becomes number two tourist attraction in state

1994 June 6 D-Day fiftieth anniversary re-enactment at Montrose Beach, Chicago, draws one million spectators

1995 Peak year for Chicago beaches attendance: 31 million people visit beaches during summer season

1999 Filming of *The Beach* takes place on the beach of Phi Phi Le Island, Thailand

2000 Beaches at Darling Harbour in Sydney, Australia, are the venue of volleyball competition in the twenty-seventh Olympic Games

Picture Credits

The photographs in this book are from the following sources and are used with permission:

FRONTISPIECE: Jantzen, Inc. **TITLE PAGE:** Christy Ottaviano collection. **DEDICATION:** Donald Van Steenwyk. **INTRODUCTION:** xii, Chicago Park District; xiii, Tony Johnston; xiv, Roy Tolles; xv, Lillian Tucker. **CHAPTER 1:** 3, the Library of Virginia; 6, Scala/Art Resource, New York; 7, the Huntington Library, San Marino, California. **CHAPTER 2:** 12, Vincent Guadazno; 13, the Huntington Library, San Marino, California; 17, Ewing Galloway, Coney Island; 19, Atlantic County Historical Society; 20, courtesy of the Rosenberg Library, Galveston, Texas; 21, Wilhelmina Adams Photograph Collection/Schomburg Center for Research in Black Culture, New York Public Library, Astor, Lenox and Tilden Foundation; 22, Brown Brothers; 23, Christy Ottaviano collection; 24, Atlantic County Historical Society. **CHAPTER 3:** 28, Florida State Archives; 29, Lake County (Illinois) Museum/Curt Teich Postcard Archives; 30, author's collection; 32, Florida State Archives; 33, Lillian Tucker; 34, 35, and 36, Jantzen, Inc.; 37, Laurie and Bruce Maclin collection; 38, Jantzen, Inc.; 39, Laurie and Bruce Maclin collection; 40, Jantzen, Inc. **CHAPTER 4:** 43 and 44, Atlantic County Historical Society; 45, Lake County (Illinois) Museum/Curt Teich Postcard Archives; 46, Cannon Beach (Oregon) Chamber of Commerce; 47, Rex R. Elliott; 48, 49, and 50, Pudgy and Les Stockton; 51, Atlantic County Historical Society; 53, Lillian Tucker. **CHAPTER 5:** 55, Surfsand Resort; 57, author's collection; 58, John Clark; 59, USA Volleyball Association/John Kessel; 60, *Five Cities Times Press Recorder*; 62, courtesy of Jane Donley, Dog Beach Dog Wash; 63, City of Pismo Beach; 64, Stuart Silver; 65, *Five Cities Times Press Recorder.* **CHAPTER 6:** 67, the Library of Virginia; 71, Atlantic County Historical Society; 73, courtesy of the American Heritage Center, reprinted with permission from Montgomery Ward; 74, Lake County (Illinois) Museum/Curt Teich Postcard Archives; 76, *Five Cities Times Press Recorder*; 77, from the archives of the San Luis Obispo County Historical Society and Museum; 78, the Huntington Library, San Marino, California; 80, Jantzen, Inc. **CHAPTER 7:** 82, 83, 84, and 85, Coney Island; 87, Utah State Historical Society; 89, Stuart Silver; 90, Laurie and Bruce Maclin Collection; 92, Zimmerman Agency, Tallahassee, Florida; 93, Florida State Archives. **CHAPTER 8:** 96, Provincetown (Massachusetts) Chamber of Commerce; 98, Fine Arts Museums of San Francisco, Mildred Anna Williams Collection (1942.7); 99, Reginald Marsh, *Coney Island Beach*/Museum of the City of New York (83.154.2); 101, author's collection; 102; Vicki Gold Levi collection; 103, courtesy of the Academy of Motion Picture Arts and Sciences and MGM Clip and Still © 1963 F.P. Productions. **CHAPTER 9:** 105, Lake County (Illinois) Museum/Curt Teich Postcard Archives; 106, National Park Service, Gateway NRA, Sandy Hook; 108, the Library of Virginia; 110, Chicago Park Service; 113, John Clark; 114, Florida State Archives; 115, Martha Tolles collection. **CHAPTER 10:** 118 and 119, *Five Cities Times Press Recorder*; 120, Sherry Shahan; 121, Lillian Tucker; 122, Sherry Shahan (both photos); 124, Florida State Archives; 125, Lillian Tucker.

Bibliography

BOOKS

BEAUFORT, DUKE OF, ED. *The Badminton Library.* London: Longmans Green & Co., 1893.

BLUME, MARY. *Cote d'Azur.* New York: Thames and Hudson, 1992.

BREWSTER, B. CHRIS, ED. *The United States Lifesaving Association Manual of Open Water Lifesaving.* Englewood Cliffs, N.J.: Prentice-Hall, 1995.

CAMERON, SILVER DONALD. *The Living Beach.* Toronto: Macmillan Canada, 1998.

CARROLL, NICK, ED. *The Next Wave: The World of Surfing.* New York: Abbeville Publishers, 1991.

CARSON, RACHEL. *The Edge of the Sea.* Boston: Houghton Mifflin, 1955.

COHN, DAVID L. *The Good Old Days.* New York: Simon & Schuster, 1940.

COOKE, JEAN, ANN KRAMER, AND THEODORE ROWLAND-ENTWISTLE. *History's Timeline.* New York: Barnes & Noble Books, 1996.

CROSS, GARY. *A Social History of Leisure.* State College, Pa: Venture Publishing, 1990.

FLACELIERE, ROBERT. *Daily Life in Greece.* New York: Macmillan, 1959.

FUNNELL, CHARLES E. *By the Beautiful Sea.* New York: Alfred A. Knopf, 1975.

GRANT, KIMBERLY. *Cape Cod and the Islands.* Woodstock, Vt.: Countryman Press, 1997.

GRIFFIN, AL. *Step Right Up Folks*. Chicago: Henry Regnery, 1974.

HALL, CARRIE A. *From Hoopskirts to Nudity*. Caldwell, Idaho: Caxton Printers, 1938.

KAUFMAN, WALLACE, AND ORRIN PILKEY. *The Beaches Are Moving*. Garden City, N.Y.: Anchor Press, Doubleday, 1979.

KRAUZER, STEVEN M. *Kayaking: Whitewater and Touring Basics*. New York: W. W. Norton, 1995.

LAVER, JAMES. *Taste and Fashion*. London: George G. Harrap and Co., 1937.

LEATHERMAN, STEPHEN P. *America's Best Beaches*. Paw Creek, N.C.: Coastal Publications, 1998.

LENCEK, LENA, AND GIDEON BOSKER. *The Beach*. New York: Penguin Putnam Group, 1998.

———. *Making Waves*. San Francisco: Chronicle Books, 1989.

LEVI, VICKI GOLD, AND LEE EISENBERG. *Atlantic City*. Berkeley, Calif.: Ten Speed Press, 1979.

MARTIN, RICHARD, AND HAROLD KODA. *Splash! History of Swimwear*. New York: Rizzoli, 1990.

MORGAN, DALE L. *The Great Salt Lake*. Indianapolis and New York: Bobbs-Merrill, 1947.

NORBURN, A. E. *Book of Bath*. Colchester, London: Ballantine Press, 1925.

OLSON, ANN S., ED. *At the Water's Edge*. Tampa: Tampa Museum of Art, 1989.

ORME, NICHOLAS. *Early British Swimming, 55 B.C.–A.D. 1719*. Exeter, England: University of Exeter, 1983.

PILAT, OLIVER, AND JO RANSON. *Sodom by the Sea*. Garden City, N.Y.: Doubleday, 1941.

SIEBERT, TED. *The Art of Sandcastling*. Seattle: Romar Books, 1990.

SMYTH, CAROLE, AND RICHARD SMYTH. *Sand Pails and Other Sand Toys*. Huntington, N.Y.: Carole Smyth Antiques, 1996.

STEELE, VALERIE. *Fashion and Eroticism*. New York: Oxford University Press, 1985.

THOREAU, HENRY DAVID. *Cape Cod*. New York: Bramhall House, by arrangement with W. W. Norton, 1951.

VAN STEENWYK, ELIZABETH. *Saddlebag Salesmen*. New York: Franklin Watts, 1995.

Zim, Herbert S., and Lester Ingle. *Seashores*. New York: Golden Books, 1989.

MAGAZINES

Watson, Bruce. "Three's a Crowd, They Say, But Not at Coney Island!" *Smithsonian,* vol. 27, no. 9 (December 1996).

PLAYS

Shakespeare, William. *Caesar and Cleopatra*. Vol. 34 in *The Dramatic Works of Shakespeare*. London, 1802.

Associations

American Kiteflyers Association
352 Hungerford Drive
Rockville, MD 20850

Cape Cod National Seashore
99 Marconi Site Road
Wellfleet, MA 02667

International Sand Collectors
    Society
P.O. Box 117
North Haven, CT 06473-0117

Scuba Diving Magazine
http://www.scubadiving.com

Surfrider Foundation USA
122 S. El Camino Real, #67
San Clemente, CA 92672

The United States Lifesaving
    Association
P.O. Box 366
Huntington Beach, CA 92648

USA Volleyball Association
715 South Circle
Colorado Springs, CO 80910

Index

(Page numbers in *italic* refer to illustrations.)